SACRED AND PROFANE MEMORIES

SACRED AND PROFANE

MEMORIES

BY
CARL VAN VECHTEN

Essay Index Reprint Series

BOOKS FOR LIBRARIES PRESS
FREEPORT, NEW YORK

PS 3543
A653 Z5

INTERNATIONAL STANDARD BOOK NUMBER:
0-8369-2337-5

LIBRARY OF CONGRESS CATALOG CARD NUMBER:
75-156727

PRINTED IN THE UNITED STATES OF AMERICA

For

Carrie and Florine Stettheimer

and

Henrie Waste

FOREWORD

The papers included in this collection have been garnered from books long out of print and from the files of yesteryear's periodicals. They have, however, been selected and arranged to create a homogeneous impression: they all deal with " things remembered." All of these papers have been rewritten, some of them extensively, but in every instance I have striven to preserve the original mood, removing only what time has taught me to believe are excrescences, adding only what may serve to accentuate my primal intention or at any rate to clarify it. Certainly, these papers are not to be regarded as essays in my contemporary manner.

Au Bal Musette and An Interrupted Conversation first appeared in The Merry-Go-Round. The Folksongs of Iowa, The Holy Jumpers, and La Tigresse are salvaged from In the Garret. How Mr. George Moore Rescued a Lady from Embarrassment was printed in the Trend. The Tin Trunk [1] was published in the Reviewer, The Night-

[1] It proved rather long for one number and was divided in two. The first part, published in the Reviewer for November 1921, bore the title at present employed; the second, published in the Reviewer for December of the same year, was entitled An Old Daguerreotype. It is interesting to record that Mr. James Branch Cabell was acting as editor of the Reviewer during both these months.

FOREWORD

ingale and the Peahen in Rogue, Notes for an Autobiography in the Colophon, and A Note on Breakfasts in the American Mercury. Feathers was one of the Random House Prose Quartos and is reprinted by permission of that publishing house. July–August 1914 has not hitherto been published anywhere, although it has existed in one form or another since October 1914. The footnotes are afterthoughts of 1931.

CARL VAN VECHTEN

New York.
August 4, 1931.

CONTENTS

ILLUSTRATIONS

"Je me souviens

Des jours anciens

Et je pleure."

PAUL VERLAINE

THE TIN TRUNK

THE TIN TRUNK

On rainy days there was always the tin trunk. My mother used to lift it down from the topmost shelf of the darkest closet in the old house, standing on a chair in order to reach it. It was not, to be precise, a trunk at all, but a tin box about ten inches wide, fifteen inches long, and perhaps five inches deep. Nevertheless, it was always called the tin trunk. Everybody, I suppose, that is everybody who retains some small grain of sentimental interest in the past, guards some such repository. In *our* box my mother preserved old letters, the rarest old letters, written to honour various family celebrations, old pictures, specifically daguerreotypes (the more recent photographs were permitted to accumulate in a large drawer in the base of one of our massive black walnut bookcases with their folding glass doors, the one, I think, which contained the complete bound file of the Atlantic Monthly,[1] to which periodical my father had been a subscriber from the first issue), clips of hair from family heads, old jewelry, most of it broken,

[1] On one occasion, when I was about six years old, contemplating a copy of this periodical on the sitting-room table, I burst into tears; nor could I be comforted. My explanation, between sobs, was: Some day I'll grow up and begin to like magazines without pictures.

I

even old pieces of dress material from favourite gowns. Each object had its own history and my mother used to relate these histories to me while I pored over the contents of the box, handling each object as gently and reverently as if it had been a religious relic and I a devout Catholic. I was a careful child and held the past in such honour that I believe, had there been a fire, I should have tried to rescue the trunk before I looked out for my own belongings.

To begin with, there was a piece of rucked vellum, folded several times and now stiff and impossible to unfold. This was an old deed of sale which in its present form had survived the fire in my grandfather's warehouse in Michigan, and had been preserved in its warped condition as a curious memento of the disaster. No bit of writing was visible on its surface. That was all *inside* and never could be read again for the flames had baked the vellum until it could no longer be unfolded. This fact was undeniably in favour of the interest of the specimen, to my child's mind one of the superior treasures of the collection, for I could imagine that it concealed a prophetic message from the past, written perhaps in my grandfather's clear but convolute hand or perhaps, and this alternative was pleasanter to dwell upon, inscribed with strange, cabalistic characters, Arabian letters, or Egyptian hieroglyphs. Now I know too well that this old rucked vellum was a deed of sale, covering the three hundred odd acres of land my grandparents had wrested from the wilderness in 1837. The document bore the signature, my uncle has since informed me, of Martin Van Buren.

There was a fragment of a charming taffeta dress, tan with little sprigs of pink and blue flowers. This was a piece of the material of my mother's wedding-dress. I knew this because the dress itself still lay in an old chest and occasionally I was allowed to see it, even to lift it so that I might smell its lavender-scented folds. When my sister was married in accordion-plaited ivory tulle, with a wide cape-collar, in the fashion of the early nineties, my mother once more donned her own wedding-dress. There were scraps of other costumes, the histories of which I do not recall, if they were ever related to me. Some of these I recognized from the silk quilts which my maternal grandmother made interminably, utilizing the dresses of half a century in forming their stars and diamonds and squares, for after my grandfather died, when I was five years old, and the old Michigan farm, whither he had come from New York as a pioneer, had been sold, my grandmother came to live with us and she occupied her declining years in fashioning silk quilts and rag rugs. At one time when Brussels and Axminster carpets were tacked to all the floors of the old house, two or three of these oval rugs were to be found in almost every room, usually in front of the fireplaces and in the doorways. They did not resemble the modern dyed rag rugs. The materials retained their natural sombre colours as befitted woollens and such utilitarian stuffs. My grandmother, who died when I was eleven years old, smoked a pipe and prophesied that I would die on the gallows.

My paternal grandmother stayed with us longer. She was almost a hundred years old, indeed, when she died, having lived through the greater part of the nineteenth century. I can still see her as she used to sit, hour after hour, silently with folded arms in the bow-window of her room on the second storey of my uncle's white brick house. Her strong will kept her alive. I photographed her sitting in her window very much in the same attitude as that in which Whistler painted his mother, but at the time I made the photograph I had not even seen a reproduction of the picture. Whistler knew that old women sit thus grimly waiting for the end, but never welcoming it, and that feeling is in my photograph of my grandmother. Some days, as a very young boy, I would go to my grandmother and read aloud to her, usually, I think, from the travel books of Bayard Taylor. They did not interest me very much and I doubt if they interested her at all, for she expressed very little curiosity concerning the strange countries which she had never visited, but it was a matter of indifference to her what I chose to read. It was my presence, *any* presence, that she desired. She dreaded being alone. It was my own idea that these would be books suitable to impress the mind of an elderly person and so I did not read to her out of my own favourite books, the works of J. T. Trowbridge, which

GRANDMOTHER VAN VECHTEN
from a photograph by Carl Van Vechten

doubtless would have pleased her more than the works of Bayard Taylor. She had a curiously gruesome mind. My cousin, Mary Van Vechten, was an excellent pianist. One day while she was practising one of Schubert's Impromptus, grandmother leaned over the banisters to call down to her: Play funeral dirges, Mary. A few days later, she gave in, her will crumbled, and she died within a few hours.

There were other objects in the tin trunk, so many, indeed, that it was necessary to bind the box with a leather thong because the clasp was weak and the cover did not close tightly. There was a chain woven from Aunt Emma's hair when it was a warm chestnut colour, perhaps when she married my father's brother, Uncle Giles, in her thirteenth year, and attached to this chain a locket with a strand of her husband's hair. I am not certain of the exact period during which hair ornaments were fashionable, but hair jewelry still persists in little second-hand shops in the city and only recently in Paris I saw many hats trimmed with hair flowers. So are pleasant modes revived.

There was a booklet in which had been printed all the letters of congratulation, of which several were in verse, sent to my mother's mother and father on the occasion of their golden wedding. An old beaded bag contained a tiny sampler embroidered by my father at the age of ten. There was a silver dollar of the year 1880, the year of my birth, with a hole through it, so that, attached to a ribbon round my throat, I had worn it as a baby. There was a tiny band of chased gold that I had worn on my finger at the same period. Among the letters, too, there was a bundle that belonged to me. When I was born my mother contracted with her younger brother who, it has always seemed to me, should have lived in the eighteenth century, so quaint his quality and so rich his flavour, to write me a letter each Christmas until I should be twenty-one. He possessed a special talent for writing letters, but such a bargain is always irksome and in almost the first letter he began to complain of this duty and by the time I was able to read them each letter was one long lamentation. After I had reached the age of twenty-one, no longer compelled by a promise, my uncle began to write to me much more frequently in an easier vein, but since my twenty-first birthday I have never received a letter from him on Christmas and I am inclined to believe that the memory of the burden still haunts his holidays.[1]

The greater part of the tin box was filled with daguerreotypes and tintypes. The latter were mostly of my sister Emma[2] and my brother Ralph,[3] a thin, serious-looking boy in his youth who passed his spare time in practising the violin and in printing. With three other boys, who performed on other instruments, he played second violin in trios and quartets and, at the age of fifteen, on his own hand-press, he printed about two dozen numbers of a

[1] Died 1930.   [2] Died 1930.   [3] Died 1927.

THE TIN TRUNK

magazine called The Rounce, most of the material for
which he actually wrote himself, but, early in life he
was swallowed up in one of my uncle's banks and he has
remained in a bank ever since. As a lad I shared his bed
for a time, but he was eighteen years older than I and, until
I had grown up, we were never very intimate. By the time
I began to enjoy looking through the tin trunk he had married and was living in a house of his own. He gave very gay
parties there; at least they seemed so to me at the time.
No intoxicating drinks of any nature ever appeared on my
father's table and it was at my brother's that I learned to
drink beer. I have since been told that the morning after
the bachelor dinner which preceded his wedding — it happened to be Sunday — I was discovered by early church-
goers marching up and down the lawn, my bare arms and
legs covered with paper bands from beer-bottles. Knowledge of smoking came much later, although I experimented
with cornsilk cigarettes behind the barn and stole a cubeb
or two from my sister who smoked them to relieve her
asthma.

My sister, a roly-poly, curly-headed blonde of six or
seven, posed for a tintype with a great shaggy dog which
must have been a Newfoundland or some approximate
breed. Later, I learned that he was named Schneider after
the dog in Joseph Jefferson's popular play, Rip Van Winkle.
Whenever I examined this picture I would inquire petu-
lantly why I was not permitted to possess a dog and my

mother would patiently explain for the hundredth time that my sister had owned Schneider when the family was living on the Michigan farm belonging to my grandfather, adding that it was more difficult to keep dogs in the city. My father, indeed, although he was the kindest-hearted of men, believed that he could not tolerate the noise and smell of an animal in the house. My first and more permanent passion had been for cats, but after I was ten years old I did not enjoy a cat's companionship until I had a home of my own. After a great deal of pleading, however, I was permitted to bring a dog into the house. She was a fox-terrier named Peg Woffington, a present from my brother who owned the bitch from whom she was bred. She died, having been poisoned, in my mother's lap, shortly after I went to college and my mother wrote me about it, a most touching letter, for mother was as much attached to Peg as I was. She was my only dog. My mother loved all animals and her heart ached when I hunted birds' eggs, for I passed through the postage-stamp, cigarette-picture, tobacco-tag, birds'-egg collecting phases, along with most of the other boys I knew. I was always collecting something, but of my juvenile collections I now miss most the cigarette pictures of coeval actresses of which I have retained too few. When I sought birds' eggs, my mother, picturing the despair of the mother bird, begged me to leave at least one egg in each nest I despoiled, but after a visit to my cousin, Roy Fitch, who

MY MOTHER
from an old ambertype

was almost professional in his attitude towards ornithology, I followed his example and collected " clutches." I climbed the tallest trees for the eggs of the scarlet tanager, scaled sandy heights for the eggs of the cliff swallow, digging deep into the sand to uncover the nests, and waded through marshes for the eggs of the bronzed grackle. Whatever little I know about nature I learned in those years.

Deprived of dogs and cats (for Peg only came to me when I was eighteen), I experimented with other fauna. I kept pigeons in the barn until they were shot on their flights by a neighbour who aimed his air-gun at any cluster of feathers lest it should build a nest in the vines which climbed up the walls of his red brick house. He did not distinguish between pigeons and English sparrows, his natural enemies. Somebody brought me an alligator from Florida, but the little reptile did not live very long. With chameleons I had more success. At different times I had under my protection field-mice, a baby thrush, and a great snapping turtle who lived in the swill-barrel, and almost all the time canaries sang in our bow-windows. My first pet at college was a little brown pig whose hoofs slipped on the polished floors when he came squealing to the door to greet me.

Daguerreotypes occupied most of the space in the tin trunk. There were not so many of these, but most of them were framed in elaborate cases, one or two of which were of deeply carved wood. I do not remember all of these, but there was a ferrotype of my father, taken, I should say, when he was about twenty, which I cannot forget. He was sitting in his shirt-sleeves, in profile. His hair and his beard were blond. There was a spiritual, even a mystic quality about this picture and I always think of it when I read Peter Ibbetson. The picture, however, I loved most, set in a tiny, oval, plum-coloured velvet case, represented my mother at eighteen, an exquisite, roguish portrait which might have been that of a Parisian beauty of the Second Empire. The honest eyes, full of character, were black and round and full, with a suggestion of witchery playing over their surface. The black hair, parted in the middle over the forehead, was smooth and glossy. The nose was strong, but not too strong, and the lips seemed to quiver with interest and emotion. A ruched bonnet, trimmed with black lace, was tied with a flowing bow under the chin. I possess many other photographs, daguerreotypes, and miniatures of my mother, made at different periods, but no other portrait of her means as much to me as this ambertype.

I remember my mother as she used to sit at the piano, the old Gilbert square rosewood grand, one of the earliest pianos to be manufactured in this country, and which today belongs to me,[1] playing a piece of which I do not recall the name, if I ever knew it, but even then it was

[1] This piano is now appropriately installed in my Victorian room which grew up around it. It miraculously preserves its

MY FATHER
from an old ferrotype

limpid, faded, sentimental music, and now as I recapture the melody it seems no more so. Sometimes she played the Rosebud Polka from sheets of music with a chromolithograph cover design of a plump girl in a short dress of écru muslin and a great straw hat tied with maroon ribbons. Sometimes she played the Rachel Polka, a jingling polka redowa. There was a chromolithograph on this cover too of the famous actress in the rôle of Phèdre wearing a harassed look under her gilt crown while she clutched her purple robes. I did not know who she was at first and for some obscure reason I refrained from asking for a long time, but I always knew that the picture and the music were incongruous. I never should have composed a polka about this tragic lady, of that I was certain. In the eighties, my sister played the Anna Song from Nanon and one day she brought home the news that Chopin had written a beautiful funeral march. I bought this march and learned to play it in my fashion, but several years passed before I discovered that this was a movement from a sonata and several more before I learned what a sonata was.

My mother had known Lucy Stone in her college days and she espoused the cause of women's suffrage at a time when the movement was most unpopular. The Woman's Journal always lay on our sitting-room table, along with Harper's Weekly and the Atlantic Monthly. She gave

---

tone and Myra Hess has honoured it by gently tapping Mozart and Scarlatti from its keys.

talks on oriental rugs at women's clubs throughout the state and perhaps was responsible for a needed improvement in Iowa taste. She was also responsible for the public library in our town, raising the sum required by Carnegie before he would build a library, and securing from state and city government sufficient income for its continued support. Nevertheless, she was in no sense of the word a public character. Her home was her one real interest. All my early life centred around her. At the time I was collecting postage stamps she brought boxes of letters, which my father had written before and during the Civil War, down from the garret and I clipped the obsolete green and blue oblongs from the corners of the envelopes. Observing me, my father, sentimental but shy of showing it, demanded that the letters be burned and burned they were while my mother wept softly, for she could not bear the idea of their being destroyed. Now I regret that they were burned and wish I had them back, for they were filled with a discussion of old matters that it would be pleasant to read about today, and some of them were love-letters, and I should like to know how my father made love to my mother.

Another day she brought down from the garret a stack of Godey's Lady's Books. The series was for the year 1868 and each number contained a folding plate, in colours applied by hand, of the fashions for the month. It was an epoch of toques and sacques. Hoops were just going out,

MY MOTHER'S PIANO IN THE VICTORIAN ROOM
from a photograph by Drix Duryea

but bustles had not yet supplanted them. The ladies in the plates were magnificent in their purple, green, and rose elegance, their dresses ornately decorated with chains, tassels, buttons, buckles, artificial flowers, embroidery, braid, ruffles, frills, ruching, lace, ribbons, bows, bugles, and passementerie. I cut these ladies out to employ them as actresses in my miniature theatre.

For this theatre I painted flies and wings which were held in place by an elaborate system of wooden blocks. There were no back drops. I manipulated the characters myself from behind, the while I spoke their lines for them. Usually I invented simple dramas, improvising the dialogue as I progressed, but on one occasion, I recall, discovering an old libretto of William Vincent Wallace's Maritana, probably a relic of an appearance of Emma Abbott at the local Greene's Opera House, I went through a good part of the lines of this opus. Owing to my complete ignorance of the music, even the much admired Scenes That Are Brightest, I was obliged to extemporize the songs. At these entertainments there was always one spectator, a neighbour's boy named Edward Howell, who lived two doors away in a house with a stuffed bird of paradise in the parlour bow-window. He enjoyed the shows sufficiently to come whenever he was invited. He was frequently my companion in the gallery of the opera house too.

My interest in the theatre developed early, but when

I was a child I liked shows better than plays: the Hanlon Brothers' extravaganzas, Superba and Fantasma, The Devil's Auction, and Wang, but I saw Richard Mansfield in Beau Brummel before I was ten, and not much later Sol Smith Russell in Peaceful Valley, Otis Skinner and Maud Durbin in Romeo and Juliet, Walker Whiteside, Clay Clement, Tim Murphy, Roland Reed and Isadore Rush, Ned Harrigan in Old Lavender, and Maggie Mitchell, a star whom my father remembered from his boyhood, in The Little Maverick. I still recall her, as the girl of the plains, bouncing up and down on an upholstered chair. Later, very much later, indeed, in New York I met her as a dear old lady, and a very rich one, I was told. I must have seen Emily Bancker in Our Flat nearly every year. Who was Emily Bancker? No one I ask ever knows and yet she was noted enough to have her picture included in the series that was given away with Sweet Caporal Cigarettes. I never saw Minnie Maddern in Fogg's Ferry or Caprice, but she was a favourite with my brother.

My mother seldom went into the kitchen save to give orders, but I was always pleading with her to cook, for she was mistress of the secrets of old-fashioned American dishes of which our Bohemian cooks were ignorant. Indian pudding was one of these and salt-rising bread another. I used to beg for this for weeks before my mother, protesting the while that it was too much trouble, would make it. I have never lost my taste for this bread and even the odour of it is still delicious to me. Many a time I have watched my mother compose this bread: I remember how she put several heaping spoonfuls of newly ground middlings with soda and boiling water, stirring the mixture well together until it nearly filled the cup. This she set over night in a warm place. It was essential that a consistent temperature be maintained and many a setting went awry because the kitchen fire went out. In the morning she put flour enough for the bread into a bread pan, adding salt and boiling water and stirring slowly. Then she added cold water and the middlings and continued to stir. In a little while the inspissated dough could be cut into loaves, into which she slashed deep gashes to assist it in rising. When the dough was light enough she put the loaves in the oven.

I loved to remain in the kitchen when my mother was cooking, but my behaviour was not always impeccable. Once, in a fury at not compelling her immediate attention, I snatched a knife from her by the blade and my palm still bears the scar of the deep ensuing cut. A similar perversity drove me to grasp potted plants by their stems and to dash them to the floor. I hated interference, objections of any kind. Orders and habits irked me. My mother was sad when my brother married and left home, as are all mothers when they similarly lose their sons. I was about seven years old at the time, but I was privy to her melancholy. Requested, that night, as usual, to go to bed at eight o'clock, I rebelled, weeping and pleading. Finally, I threatened: If you don't let me stay up, I'll marry!

It gives me a curious sensation to make a list of my childhood memories. I recall vividly such seemingly unimportant details. Are the memories of ghosts made up of such stuff? I wonder. I can remember very clearly a Christmas tree, my first, at Aunt Emma's, when I was two years old, and just where the tree stood in the big bow-window of her dining-room. I can remember a packwax party at Addie Lawton's on Third Avenue and how we dropped the boiling maple syrup into bowls stuffed tight with snow so that it hardened and cooled sufficiently to be eaten with the fingers, and I still can recall the texture and the taste, although I do not believe I have eaten any packwax for thirty years. I can remember donning my first pair of knickerbockers at the age of six. I cried and did not want to wear them to school, for I had always worn kilts, all my friends still wore kilts, and change is abhorrent to youth. A little girl, a family connection, came sometimes to visit us from a neighbouring town. When the house was too crowded to permit of her sleeping alone she was put into my bed. I can remember the night when we were told that we were too old to sleep together any longer. We did not understand why and we did not like the injunction. As a matter of fact she joined me in bed before the night was over. We had both been crying, what with the strangeness of the new order and because we had been reading Puss-Cat-Mew together and the memory of its horrible ogres terrified us. We were not aware of the existence of The Mysteries of Udolpho or The Castle of Otranto. Had we been we should have read them, for we revelled in the horror school. We did discover a story about a nyctalope, the name of which I have forgotten, but the effect of which was so terrifying that we slept with the gas burning for three nights. We often played in the garden, arranged in crosses and crescents and circles of old-fashioned posies. There were pinks and asters and marigolds, hollyhocks, sweet elysium, nasturtiums, mignonette, sweet peas, and pansies, and a row of aromatic yellow roses blooming on bushes my mother had brought from Michigan. In the spring there was a great bed of lilies of the valley and another of violets. In February, or even earlier, my father sent for all the seed-catalogues and we examined these together. My father was very proud of his lawn. He gave me a penny for every twenty-five weeds I pulled. An aged Negro named Mr. Oliphant worked all the time at this task. My father preferred huge brown scars in the lawn to weeds. Rain water was collected in a cistern and that had to be pumped into a tank in the attic so that we might have soft water for bathing. It was not until after I had gone away to college that an electric pump was installed. One of the unpleasant memories of my childhood is that of my daily turn at the pump.

SACRED AND PROFANE MEMORIES

When, at the age of thirteen, I was taken to the World's Fair at Chicago, I spent most of my time alone on the Midway Plaisance watching the oriental dancing, novel to most Americans of the period and absolutely enthralling to me. The lady who could make an apple bound and bounce about by the movements of her abdomen especially delighted me. One day some kinswoman without an escort carried me away from the pleasures of the Plaisance to the Art Gallery. The only pictures I saw that day which I still remember were Corot's Orpheus and a painting by Bouguereau called, I fancy, Invading Cupid's Realm, which fascinated me, perhaps, because until then I had seen comparatively few pictures of naked women.

The eighties and nineties, the years of my boyhood, were passed far away from Jules Laforgue and César Franck, Erik Satie, Stéphane Mallarmé, Paul Verlaine, Oscar Wilde, and Aubrey Beardsley. I had never heard of The Yellow Book, but I was well acquainted with The Chap Book, published by Stone and Kimball at Chicago. I devoured all the books I could find, but I began by adoring J. T. Trowbridge and Horatio Alger, Jr. I did not care for Oliver Optic and G. A. Henty, but Ingersoll Lockwood's fanciful tales delighted me. So did those of Frank Stockton. They still do: The Bee-Man of Orn and The Floating Prince occupy very important positions in my library. I loved to wander through old copies of St. Nicholas and Wide Awake. I read The Swiss Family Robinson, an abbreviated version of The Arabian Nights, and the Baron Munchausen in the edition illustrated by Gustave Doré. I even liked Little Lord Fauntleroy and Sara Crewe. Then, for a time I switched to Nick Carter and Golden Days. This addiction annoyed my father. I wonder why: I should give them to my son today, had I the son and the periodicals. With Dickens, Richard Harding Davis, Mark Twain, Shakespeare, and yes, Ibsen, a new orgy of reading commenced. I read everything that I could find in the house, but I seldom borrowed books. Perhaps it was my appetite for reading that inspired my mother to found the Free Public Library in our town. When that was opened with the beautiful Virginia Dodge as librarian few limitations were put on my fancy. I read What Maisie Knew, fresh from the new press of Stone and Kimball, Daudet's Sapho, and, somewhat later, two books which made an indelible impression on me: The Confessions of a Young Man and Plays Pleasant and Unpleasant.

My mother wore a turkey-red shawl and amethysts and topazes set in long bar brooches. Our neighbour's son, Redmond Stevens, rode a high bicycle. My first bicycle was of the more modern, low variety, which insured one against the possibility of taking a header. Occasionally Crazy Hen made one of his mad parades down the street. I rose before dawn to meet the circus-train, following the canvas-covered wagons and the elephants up the silent, deserted streets to the ball-park. The other mornings on which I got out of bed in the darkness were the Fourth of July and Christmas. My sister sewed musk-mellon seeds in designs of stars and daisies on bands of black velvet for collars. Later, she began to carve wood and cut deep designs in cabinets and chairs and chests. Whole rooms in our house were furnished with her work at one time. At first she polished the wood, but she soon learned that this was the mark of machine-made furniture and thereafter she oiled it. My brother's wife, Fannie, painted china and brought the first kiln to our town so that she could fire her own porcelain after she had painted it. The first time she used the kiln the clay stilts supporting the china were not properly placed and after the fire was extinguished and the oven opened all the china was found to be broken. However, she was never again unsuccessful. Every morning, Theodore, my uncle's hired man, carried a pail of milk to us from my uncle's Jersey cow. He never bought a suit of clothes, never, indeed, spent a penny, and when my uncle died Theodore was a rich man, but when he stopped work he took to his bed, and he too passed away in a few months. In our barn there were posters of the Hanlons in the Voyage en Suisse, Rhea in Josephine, Empress of the French, James O'Neill on a rock uttering the famous " The world is mine! " speech in Monte Cristo, and Frank Mayo in the leggings and fur cap of David Crockett. There were pictures, too, of The Corsican Brothers and Eugene Aram . . . or was it Enoch Arden? It is extraor-

dinary, George Moore has said, how we can be transported into the past — in thought. Everything is thought,
all begins in thought and all returns to thought. Life is so
illusory that it is hard to say whether we live in the past
or the present or the future. . . . I sit before the fire and
study the old ambertype of my mother, so like a belle of
the Second Empire. . . .

March 18, 1921.

THE FOLKSONGS OF IOWA

THE FOLKSONGS OF IOWA

I

Of late years those interested in such matters have expended considerable energy searching for folksongs in America. Stimulated, no doubt, by the example of England, a country which not so very long ago believed herself folksongless, but which discovered to her own astonishment that she had as many folksongs as Sweden or Italy, collectors have ranged over these United States in a desperate effort to capture whatever specimens of the art of the people may still linger in what has hitherto been considered an hostile environment. The result has been that Cecil J. Sharp, in a trip through the Southern Appalachian mountains, through the states of West Virginia, Kentucky, North and South Carolina, Alabama, Tennessee, and Georgia, found this region more profitable for the collection of old English and Scottish folksongs than their original habitat. The reason for this is that in England nowadays only the old sing, and they only after much persuasion, but in the Southern mountains, far from the railroads, the young sing as well as the old: many of them have large repertories. Even before Cecil Sharp with his unusual scholarship undertook the chase, Josephine McGill had collected folksongs in the Kentucky mountains and Loraine Wyman and Howard Brockway had heard their Lonesome Tunes in the same locality. Frances Densmore discovered her Indian folksongs, published by the Bureau of Ethnology, in Minnesota. Charles F. Lummis gathered a group of cowboy songs. William Francis Allen, Charles Packard Ware, Lucy McKim Garrison, Emily Hallowell, and, more recently, Natalie Curtis Burlin and Henry Burleigh, sought to put down as many of the old Negro folksongs as possible. Mrs. Burlin, indeed, is responsible for the announcement of the fact that Negro folksongs are polyphonic, sung in harmony rather than in unison. One critic, H. E. Krehbiel, inoculated with the fancy originally, no doubt, by his friend Lafcadio Hearn, has been interested in all manifestations of folksong. His curiosity regarding the different versions of a certain ballad called The Jew's Daughter has almost amounted to a fetish. At various times he has written about Indian folksongs and he has devoted the best of his books to a discussion of the Negro song. It is perhaps unfortunate that his interest has been that of the lepidopterist who pins his butterflies to boards rather than that of the poet observer who finds his joy in watching the iridescent insects mount into the ether or, with miniature proboscides, suck the nectar from the bending foxglove. However, neither Mr. Krehbiel nor any of the others I have mentioned has thought of collecting folksongs in Iowa.

THE FOLKSONGS OF IOWA

Now there are Indian reservations in Iowa and the Bohemian in his Czech (not his ribald) form settles there in large groups. Many happy months of Dvořák's American sojourn were passed there. A legend even exists to the effect that the greater part of the Symphony From the New World was composed there. It is far from my intention, however, to intimate that he heard Swing Low, Sweet Chariot, which is suggested in this score, in this middle-western state. I was born in a town in Iowa where at least half the population is of Slavic origin and I was brought up on Bohemian lullabies. When our cook was in good humour she sang lusty Czech airs, reminiscent of foaming amber Pilzener and stamping booted feet, waving ribboned skirts, embroidered jackets, and elaborately flowered headdresses. In a different mood she crooned nostalgic melodies, plaintive in their monotony. However, the search for the Indian and Bohemian folksong in Iowa — and I am certain that here lies a rich harvest for the assiduous collector — I perforce leave to others. It occurred to me to gather in the folksongs of the Iowa farmer, the epic of the corn.

II

There are villages in New England; there are hamlets in England; in Iowa there are cities and towns. In one of the typical cities the wide streets are paved with bricks, canopied by sweeping elm branches which meet overhead like Gothic ogives. There are rows of new brick or stucco dwellings in pseudo-English or colonial style, or better still, stately, authentic 1870 Victorian mansions, identifiable by cupolas and scroll-work. The walls of many of these houses are clothed in purple or white clematis, or wistaria, or, more often, woodbine or English ivy. In the gardens, day lilies, roses, gladioli, and bleeding-hearts bloom. On every hand you will observe an attempt at amateur landscape gardening with here a syringa, there a flaming mountain ash, here a clump of lilac bushes, there a tub of blue hydrangeas. This vegetation is clean-cut, attended-to, matter-of-fact, and the buildings themselves, whether residences or outhouses, give the same impression of prosperity. So do the city parks, particularly that facing the railroad station, with the name of the town embroidered in coleus and cockscombs on a sloping bank of well-clipped grass, suggesting a giant's grave. Churches, schools, libraries, theatres, moving-picture auditoriums, rise in their magnificence on every side, nor are business blocks lacking, multifloored business blocks with elevators. Slightly removed from the main thoroughfares, factories flaunt their gaunt stacks. Motor-cars, Fords, Cadillacs, and Packards, line the streets along the curbs, buzz along the numbered streets and avenues. I believe there are more automobiles in this Iowa city than there are in Monte Carlo. The very atmosphere exudes good fortune, a certain animal comfort, and also, unfortunately, a certain smugness. This then is an Iowa city, entirely itself in its newly painted freshness, its up-to-date air, the greenness of its foliage, and the striking self-satisfaction of its inhabitants, but also sedulously aping corners in Paris, nooks in Oxford, walls in Beaune, gardens at Hampton Court, country clubs at Rye, churches at Siena, farmhouses at Ronda, and banks at Chicago. This could be no fitting spot for the study of the folksong. In this environment one might only expect to hear the music of Irving Berlin or Richard Strauss, of Louis A. Hirsch or Puccini.

So one very hot Iowa day — and hot days in Iowa are hotter and brighter than one can experience elsewhere west of Verona or east of Arizona — I set forth from this pleasant city in one of the few buggies which remained from the civilization of the eighties or the nineties, a civilization completely brushed aside in such a community by the rude rush of modernity. There is indeed more of the Rome of the Empire in the Rome of today than there is of the Iowa town of 1870 in the Iowa city of today. A not too loquacious driver lounged informally in his shirt-sleeves on the ample front seat of the buggy and I sat in the back in the shelter of a black leather hood. Beside me on the seat I had placed a few sheets of blank music paper, a tuning fork, and an instrument capable of making phonograph records.

Iowa towns have no suburbs. You pass suddenly from the town itself into the farming country, for the towns are built compactly that they may not encroach on the fields of growing corn. It may be said that the growing of corn is the chief concern of the state. Indeed, for a certain time in the summer, the unfailing topic of conversation is the weather. Dry hot weather is essential for the successful growing of corn and the economic welfare of the community depends entirely on the corn crop. Bank stocks, the prices of dry goods and green groceries, rents and dressmakers' bills, all are affected by a bad corn year.

The Iowa scene has been infrequently described in literature and no writer, I think, has as yet done justice to it. There is, indeed, a feeling abroad that the Iowa scene is unworthy of description, as Iowa is usually imagined as a fecund but unbeautiful state laid out in flat squares. The contrary is the case. This fair land is unusually personal in its appeal and its beauty, which may not be immediately appreciated by those who glance at it casually from the back of an observation car on the Overland Limited, in the end proves to be haunting. Indeed, to me the Iowa scene boasts a peculiar picturesqueness which I do not find elsewhere in the United States. I might explain this prejudice by recalling how often Pennsylvania or Connecticut suggests England, while Iowa remains essentially American. Far from being flat, the ground is constantly rolling, so that when, as frequently happens, the eye enjoys an unhindered view of fields of corn in every direction, the light, dry wind playing over the green and tasselled stalks

in the hot sunglare, the effect is produced of the undula-
tion of the waves in a southern sea. There is, indeed, to be
found in the state of Iowa a kind of inspiration associated
with great rivers, high mountains, or that mighty monster,
Ocean, " that liest curl'd like a green serpent round about
the world."

There are other pictures which interrupt the cornfields.
Brooks abound, bubbling joyously over white-stoned, sandy
beds, across which bend willow trees. Occasionally one
encounters a copse, not a stately Michigan forest, but a
delightfully bushy congeries of trees and underbrush, an
overgrown spinney in which lindens, elms, and the comfortable maple, which later will illuminate the landscape
with all the hues of a Bakst canvas, rear their modest
heights over the heads of hazel shrub and sumac which in
turn shelter milkweed, mullein, thistle, and fern. The
shade is never intense, the copse is never cool in the summer; the warm rays of the sun penetrate the fragile covering of leaves as easily as they would the laced panels of a
sunshade held by a languid English lady on a Maidenhead
lawn. Striped chipmunks hustle and bustle among the
dead leaves that carpet the sandy soil. Field mice and toads
are friendly enemies. There are a few squirrels and rabbits.
Deer, fox, and bears have long since disappeared from a region which offers so little security to the pursued. The
scraping of the cicadas in the overheated air at times becomes a burden too terrible to be borne, until the intensity

of this rhythmic sound is unexpectedly forgotten in the lesser singing of the cricket.

The road passes over a wooden bridge, roughly railed; the boards clatter under the untired wheels of the buggy. We lean out to catch the glimmer of silver trout in the stream below and the quick flash of a mammoth dragon-fly, darning-needle is the homely name, a dragon-fly resplendent with sapphire and emerald. Now we are out of the woods and passing through acres of corn land again. There are no rail fences in Iowa, no stone walls, only barbed wire, extending tautly from post to post. On these shining wires the saucy bluebirds strut. Bronzed grackles, rose-breasted grosbeaks, scarlet tanagers, yellow warblers, and red-winged blackbirds on the blue background of the sky suggest a vast Spanish shawl. The meadowlark soars, a hawk seeking prey swoops low, and a crow calls Caw! Caw! Caw! The silly mew of the catbird strikes our ear from the neighbouring bush, the woodpecker taps on the maple tree, and the cuckoo's thieving note sounds from the distance.

We pass a farmer in his field. Is this the Iowa peasant? He guides a horse with a harrow through the straight aisles that separate the rows of corn, but he does not sing. He is silent, save when occasionally he calls out Gee up! to the beast ahead. He does not otherwise interrupt the chir-ruping of the pretty yellow warblers, the constant fiddling of the cicadas, the buzz of the locusts. Our horse neighs.

THE FOLKSONGS OF IOWA

The constant heat, serving as conductor of sound, accentuates this symphony of Nature, brings out the different voices.

Now, ahead over the brow of the hill, I actually do hear human singing. I urge my driver to make speed. He clucks to our horse and the buggy rolls rapidly on. We make the top of the hill and a few yards below its crest a schoolhouse rises. This is the source of the music. The children are singing, Good morning, merry sunshine, and as we leave the school-house behind we hear, My country, 'tis of thee.

The farm in Iowa, unlike so many farms in the South or in New England, is not untidy. The yards are not strewn with rusting machinery or rotting wheelbarrows. The farm in Iowa in its own way is as magnificent as the château in France. The house itself, it is true, is often insignificant, a simple, white, clapboarded structure, surrounded by a few shade trees, but the outlying buildings sound the true imperial note. An Artesian well or windmill, a tower of glittering steel, imitates the Tour Eiffel. The ample siloes are as imposing in their cylindrical whiteness as the turrets of a robber baron's castle on the Rhine. The barns, the stables, the hog-pens, and the chicken yards are beyond all Eastern dreams of country grandeur. The Iowa farmer accepts orders over the telephone and delivers them in his motor-truck.

Passing such a farm, we observe several men working silently in the fields. They greet us soberly. There is apparently no gaiety in the heart of the Iowa farmer. The farmer's wife, a plain, slender woman in calico, stands on the porch of her little white house, partially hidden among evergreen trees. We wave to her and she waves her hand in reply, but not with the heartiness with which she would greet a friend. I bid my man to stop the horse and, leaping out of the buggy into the road, I run lightly up the gravel path.

We don't want to buy nothin', are the lady's first words; nothin' at all.

I don't want to sell nothin', neither, I retort. Does any one here sing?

Be you a music teacher or a piano tuner? My darter sings sometimes.

No, I'm not a teacher. I like music.

The eyes of the farmer's wife wander to the spot in the yard where Towzer's kennel stands. Towzer's head protrudes, a wicked bulldog head. Towzer growls tentatively and waits for the signal. I prepare for the attack, when unexpectedly the woman decides to humour me.

Aggie! she calls. Aggie!

What is it, ma? a shrill voice from the garden demands.

Come here a minute.

In due time Aggie appears, a fat, freckled girl with hair which, in a cat show, would be called " any other colour." She is wearing a blue skirt and a red flannel dressing-sacque. In the curve of one arm she carries a pan of lima bean pods. With the other hand she fingers the tied ends of a sunbonnet.

There's a music man here, her mother explains.

I thought perhaps I could hear some singing. Don't you ever sing among yourselves.

Aggie giggles. Ma even permits her worried, wrinkled face to exhibit a slight smile. Towzer stops growling.

Just you sit on the piazza a minute, Aggie suggests coyly. . . . She passes the portal. Ma and I sit on two uncomfortable wooden rocking-chairs. I have forgotten my music paper, my tuning fork, my phonograph recording apparatus, but it is too late to go after them. Aggie touches the keys of an invisible piano. Aggie is singing, loudly and unmistakably, Aggie is singing:

> Oh — ev'ry evening hear him sing,
> It's the cutest little thing,
> Got the cutest little swing,
> Hitchy koo, hitchy koo, hitchy koo . . .

Very pretty, I gasp. Very pretty.

Come on in the parlour, Ma suggests.

We enter the low ceilinged room hung with framed chromolithographs issued as Sunday supplements to the Chicago newspapers. High in the wall in one corner is the tin stopper of the stove-pipe hole. Stove and pipe have disappeared for the summer. The furniture is early Grand Rapids and looks brand new; the carpet is red and green ingrain. The piano is black and upright. Aggie is fumbling in a music cabinet. Presently she finds what she wants and returns to the stool to sing:

From the land of the sky bloo waaa-tur . . .

Aggie's third choice is even more inspired:

Pale haaands I loved beside the . . .

So I discover a bond between Iowa and Mayfair! Did Cecil Sharp learn more in his Appalachian travels? I doubt it. I thank Aggie. I thank ma. I even toss a kind word to Towzer as I pass the kennel and hurry on to my buggy. I wake up my Sancho Panza, snoozing on the front seat, and once more we are under way.

More cornfields, more copses, more birds and butterflies, more stern and sober workers. Occasionally an automobile passes us, occasionally a wagon loaded with crates of vegetables or chickens. A fresh phenomenon is a duck yard. Hundreds of white birds are huddled together in pens with stretches of water like canals in Holland. In the next cornfield stands a quaint scarecrow clothed in blue overalls and a long frock coat with a sombrero tied with a gay red bandana on his head.

An hour later we drive up to another farmhouse to give our Rosinante food and water. My companion on the front seat drives the steed to the barn. I straightway enter the farmhouse kitchen where the gaunt housewife prepares the midday meal which is called dinner in Iowa. Nodding a curt good-day she assures me, in reply to my request, that I may share pot-luck. Tea stews in the kettle on the stove; tea is always stewed in Iowa, black and strong. Sometimes the kettle with its residue stands for days on the stove, unmolested save for the pouring out of cupfuls now and then and the replenishing of water and green tea leaves. Steaks cut as thin as sandwiches in Sutton Place are frying in the pan. Grilling is an unknown art in these regions. Vegetables are boiling in pots of milk. Watch the patient housewife as she cuts the long and splendid asparagus stalks into worm-length bits which she tosses dextrously into the hot liquid. A green head of lettuce fresh from the garden is flung into the wooden chopping bowl and soon reduced to atoms which are presently drowned in vinegar. However, during all these operations and the preparation of buckwheat griddle-cakes, there is no singing, except that furnished by the tea-kettle; nor is there much conversation, although two women are assisting the housewife. The women bustle about, but they do not talk. The farm-hands come in and eat from the heavily laden, unclothed table. Food is shovelled into the mouth without respite, but still the tongues do not speak. Occasionally some one asks a question, but the reply is usually monosyllabic. Dinner done, I ask for a song.

Song! says the farmer. We ain't got no time for songs!

A maidservant titters. So does my Sancho.

I guess the city feller's crazy, a husky voice whispers in the corner.

The farm-hands file out. I thank the housewife and attempt to settle the reckoning, but she refuses the money.

We don't take no boarders, she says, but strangers is always welcome, if there ain't too many of us eatin'. We can't take nobody in at harvest time.

Sancho inducts the steed back into the traces. The buggy starts, leaps forward into the road, and soon we have left the farmhouse far behind. The sun is lowering, the shadows fall long. Sancho turns to me confidentially.

Say, feller, speaks our squire, if you want ter hear some singin' there's a farmer over the next hill's got a pious bug. Most every day after dinner somebody's singin' hymns for an hour: Onward, Christian Soldiers, At the Cross, and all those.

Smiling feebly, I shake my head. Reluctantly I give the signal to proceed back to the city. Why is it that Natalie Burlin, Loraine Wyman, Frances Densmore, and Cecil Sharp can go out in the morning and return at night with a bundle of melodies in Mixolydian, Dorian, and Æolian modes? I recall an experience of my own in Shoreditch, an humble outlying district of London. Seeking the cheapest of the music halls, I entered to find myself surrounded by cockneys so bebuttoned that they seemed to symbolize the despoliation of the button factories, the females so befeathered that in their bedraggled way they rivalled Mistinguett. At last, I muttered to myself, I shall hear a good racy East London song. The lights were lowered; a white screen replaced the drop curtain. This was before the days of moving-pictures; an illustrated song was indicated. Presently a scrawny female in a dirty pink satin dress walked out. Tike me 'ome to owld New 'ampshire, mother dear, were the words she sang. The picture on the screen represented Times Square by moonlight.

III

The tongues of the farmers had been still; even the farmers' wives had been comparatively silent. They had not worked in the fields to the accompaniment of some broad sweeping rhythm; I had not heard a suggestion of the pentatonic scale; but, as we drove back through this splendid region, it came to me that Iowa has her own folk-songs. The melody of the yellow warbler, the soft low call of the brown thrasher, the entrancing, inspirational cry of the meadowlark mounting to heaven, the whippoorwill shouting his own name, the caw of the crow, the tap, tap, tap of the red-headed woodpecker, the shrill raucous cackle of the magisterial but quarrelsome bluejay, the heart-breaking, dirge-like moan of the mourning dove, the memory of all these confirmed my belief that Iowa has her folksongs, but the corn itself, the unserried ranks of green, tassel-bearing stalks growing, almost perceptibly

39

growing, in the hot cicada-burdened atmosphere, sings, it seems to me the noblest song of all: The corn song, beginning, no doubt, if one could transcribe it into our rude Iowa English, I am the corn! a noble line, a magnificent refrain, which is repeated as far as the eye and ear can reach.

December 19, 1918.

AU BAL MUSETTE

AU BAL MUSETTE

One July night in Paris I dined with a lady at the Cou-Cou and later we sipped our cognac at the Savoyard. I find nothing strange in this program. I must have dined at the Cou-Cou many times before with many friends, and a liqueur at the Savoyard has followed as a matter of course. To go there you take a taxicab to the foot of the Mont-martre hill and then are drawn up in the funicular railway to the top where the church of Sacré-Cœur squats proudly, for all the world like a mammoth Buddha. Of course you may ride all the way up the mountain in your taxi if you like. From Sacré-Cœur you turn to the left, following the board fence which, it would seem, will eternally hedge in this unfinished monument of pious catholics, passing on through the Place du Tertre, in which you must not be tempted to sit down with the Parisian clerks eating their petite marmite in the open air, until you arrive at the Place du Calvaire. The tables of the Restaurant Cou-Cou occupy nearly the whole of this tiny square to which there are only two means of approach, one up the stairs from the city below, the other from the Place du Tertre.[1] An artist's

[1] On July 14, 1930, nearly fifteen years after this paper was written, I was the guest of the Princess Violette Murat at a

house disturbs the view on the side towards Paris; the restaurant opposite is flanked by a row of modest apartment houses to which one gains an entrance by means of a small gate through a high wall. Sundry visitors to these houses, some on bicycles, make occasional interruptions in the dinner. From over this wall, too, comes the great tabby cat which lounges about in the hope, frequently realized, that some one will toss him the bone of a chicken. Adjoining the restaurant on the right is a tiny cottage, fronted by a still tinier garden protected by a paling. Many of the visitors to the Cou-Cou hang their hats and sticks on this fence and its gate. Not once in my numerous visits to this open air restaurant have I seen the occupants of this cottage, but on one occasion, the crowd in the square doubtless becoming too noisy, towards eleven o'clock in the evening an

---

dinner in a private room in the Savoyard. The dinner and the wines were superb. It was amusing to watch the holiday crowd below in the strong high lights of the red and green Bengal fires which illuminated Sacré-Cœur, and the fireworks on Montmartre were prettily mirrored at Montparnasse on the opposite side of the city. After dinner I strolled around to the Place du Calvaire to find the whole aspect of the place changed. The exploitation of the Place du Tertre and the picturesque side streets has filled the district with professional postcard sellers, in velours bérets and jackets, and shops where cheap souvenirs are sold. A most unattractive group is now delighted to sit at the tables which occupy all the space in the Place du Tertre. The old Montmartre has completely disappeared.

upper window was suddenly thrown open and a pailful of water was ejected.

The Place du Calvaire presents a delightful picture on a summer night when tiny lights in pink globes are placed on the tables. The square twinkles with them and the couples at the tables, the pretty girls in their bell-shaped hats with their bearded companions, become gay, and sometimes sentimental. The pink lamps are a signal for the appearance of a small boy in blue trousers who comes along to light the street lamp. Now a gang of urchins gathers on the wall, which hedges in a garden on the fourth side of the square, to utter audible and extremely uncomplimentary comments about the people who are eating.

I have described the Cou-Cou as it was this night and as it has been on all the nights during the summers I have been there. The dinner too is always the same. It is served à la carte, but one is not given much opportunity to choose. There is always a soup, spaghetti, roast chicken, and salad, invariably lobster, and zabaglione, if one desires it. The wine — it is called chianti — is tolerable. The addition is made appropriately upon a slate with a piece of white chalk. One inquires: Qu'est-ce que monsieur a mangé? Sometimes it is very difficult to remember, but it is necessary. Such complete faith calls for equally complete honesty. It is all added up and for the two of us on this evening, or any other evening, it may come to nine francs [1] which is not a great deal to pay for a good dinner.

Then, on this evening, and every other evening, we went back as we had come, rounding Sacré-Cœur, passing the statue of the Chevalier who was martyred for refusing to salute a procession — why he refused I have never learned although I have asked everybody who has ever dined with me at the Cou-Cou — to the Café Savoyard, the broad windows of which look out over pretty much all the northeast quarter of Paris, now a glittering labyrinth of lights set in an obscure sea of darkness. It was not far from here that Louise and Julien were living together when they were interrupted by Louise's mother, and it was looking down towards these lights that they swore those eternal vows, ending with Louise's C'est une féerie! and Julien's correction, Non, c'est la vie! I always recalled this scene and felt it at the Savoyard as intensely as I did when I watched Mary Garden and Léon Beyle from the topmost gallery of the Opéra-Comique after a wait of an hour and a half in the queue for one franc tickets. A great number of persons were always turned away from performances of Louise and so it was essential to be standing in line early. Some other operas did not demand such punctuality. There is a terrasse outside the Savoyard, a miniature terrasse, with just room for one man, who griddles gaufrettes, and three or four

[1] The franc at the epoch of which I write was valued at twenty cents in American money.

small tables with chairs. We sat at one of these that night
— just as I had sat so many times before — to sip our
cognac.

In recalling an adventure it is difficult to be certain just
when one broke with the past to embrace the future, but I
think the hour of destiny must have struck in this café. It
was the first time I had ever seen a cat there. In New York
he would have been an oddity, but in Paris there are many
such beasts. This lazy, splendid animal was lying on the
bar, tawny, soft, and monstrous, and as I stroked his coat
he purred mellifluously. As I lifted the animal into my
arms, the better to enjoy his warmth and softness, he
unsheathed his claws, and easily releasing himself, sprang
back to the bar. There was blood on my face, I noted in the
mirror. Madame behind the bar was apologetic, but not
chastening. Il avait peur, she explained. Il n'est pas
méchant. My wound proved to be literally a scratch, and
as I stroked the cat's fur again, he began to purr.

We decided to walk down the hill, instead of riding
down as we had come up in the funicular railway, down
the stairs which form another of the pictures in Louise,
with the abutting houses, into the rooms of which one
never can resist looking, although conscious of prying.
You see the old in these interiors, making shoes, or preparing dinner, or the middle-aged going to bed, but one
never sees the young in these houses in the summer.

It was early and we thought it would be pleasant to

dance. I recalled the Moulin de la Galette which waves its gaunt arms in the air half way up the Butte Montmartre, serving its purpose as a dance hall of the quarter. The pretty Montmartre models go there and the young artists. The entrance fee is not exorbitant and you are under no obligation to order more than a bock. When I have visited the Moulin de la Galette, sitting at a small table facing the vivid mural decoration which runs the length of one wall, drinking my brown bock, I sometimes remember the story Mary Garden once told me, how Albert Carré, to celebrate the hundredth — or was it the twenty-fifth? — performance of Louise, offered a dinner there — so near the scenes he had reproduced on the stage — to Charpentier and how, surrounded by some of the most notable musicians and poets of France, the composer had suddenly fallen from his chair, face downwards. He had starved himself so long to complete his masterpiece that food did not seem to nourish him. This was the end of these festivities. They carried him away to the Riviera. Some said he had lost his mind; some said he was dying. Mary Garden herself did not know what had happened to him when in 1910 she first sang Louise at the Manhattan Opera House in New York. A little later, however, the rumour spread that he was writing a trilogy. Still later, Julien, the second lyric drama of the trilogy was eventually produced and everybody knows the story of its failure. Charpentier, the natural philosopher and poet of Montmartre, apparently had written himself out in Louise. As for the third play, one has heard nothing more about it.[1]

On this particular evening we discovered the Moulin de la Galette to be closed, and then I recalled that it was open on Thursday and this was Wednesday. Is it Thursday, Saturday, and Sunday that the Moulin de la Galette is open? I think so. By this time we were determined to dance, but where? We had no desire to go to some dull place common to tourists. The Bal Tabarin did not lure us; nor the more plausible Grelot in the Place Blanche, for we had been there a night or two before. The Elysée Montmartre, celebrated by George Moore, would be closed. Its proprietor followed the schedule of days adopted by the Moulin de la Galette. In my perplexity I consulted a small boy who had been good enough to guide us through many winding streets to the Moulin. Certainly he knew of a bal. Would monsieur care to visit a bal musette? His companion appeared to be slightly shocked by the suggestion. I caught the phrase " mal frequenté." My curiosity was aroused and I gave the signal to advance.

I seemed to remember having read somewhere that the ladies of the court of Louis XIV played the musette, which is French for bagpipes. The fashionable instruments of an

[1] Even now in 1931 no more has been heard of it, although Charpentier was still enough alive in 1929 to attend Grace Moore's performance of Louise at the Opéra-Comique and to have his picture taken with her.

epoch, the musettes of the great ladies were elaborately decorated. In time the word slunk into the dictionaries of musical terms as a description of a drone bass. Many of Gluck's ballet airs, for example, bear the title Musette. Perhaps the bass was even originally performed on the bagpipes. . . . Mal frequenté has a variety of significations, depending on the station of the employer of the phrase. Certainly a lady and a street urchin would not have the same definition for it. In this particular instance I fancied the word implied apaches.[1] A bal attended by street-walkers or models would not be so described by a boy of the streets because all the public balls of Paris were so attended. No, the words the boy had muttered to my companion must have spelled apaches, suggesting to him a certain amount of danger. The confusion of epochs began to invite my interest and I wondered in my mind's eye, how a Louis XIV apache would dress, how he might be represented at a costume ball, and I evoked a vision of a ragged silk-betrousered person, flaunting a plaid-bellied instrument.

The two urchins lead us through street after street, one of them whistling that pleasing tune, Le lendemain elle était souriante. Dark passage ways intervened between us and our destination: we threaded them. The cobble-stones

[1] The most romantic ruffians of our times until the New York gangsters and racketeers stole some of their sordid glamour.

underfoot were not easy to walk on for my companion, shod in shoes with high heels. The boys amused both us and themselves by their capers on the way. They could have made our speed walking on their hands and they accomplished at least a third of the journey in this manner. Of course we tossed them numberless large round five and ten copper centimes pieces.

At last we arrived before a door in a short street near the Gare du Nord. Was it the Rue Jessaint? I do not know, for when, a year later, I attempted to refind this bal, it had disappeared. We could hear the hum of the pipes for some minutes before we turned the corner into the street, and never have pipes sounded in my ears with such a shrill significance of being somewhere they ought not to be, that is never except once long afterwards when I listened to the piper who accompanies the dinner of the Governor of the Bahamas in Nassau. Marching round and round the porch of the Governor's villa he played The Bluebells of Scotland and God Save the King, but, hearing these familiar sounds from a distance through the interstices of the cocoa-palm fronds in the hot tropical night, I could only think of a Hindu blowing his pipe in India to charm the cobras. So, as we turned the corner into the Rue Jessaint, I seemed to catch a faint glimpse of a scene on the lawn at Versailles. Louis XIV! It was the epoch of Cinderella!

But it wasn't bagpipes at all. That we discovered when,

after passing through the bar in front, we entered the large hall at the back of the house where the bal was conducted. In the doorway lounged a sergent de ville, always a guest at one of these functions, I discovered later. There were rows of long tables, with wooden benches placed between them. One corner of the floor was cleared for dancing — not so large a corner either — and on a small platform sat the strangest looking youth, without emotion or expression of any kind on his countenance. The bagpipes, symbol of the bal, hung disused on the wall over his head. He was playing an accordion with great skill, the sound of which was augmented and the rhythm accented by sleighbells attached to his ankles in such a manner that a minimum of movement produced a maximum of effect. He further added to the tonal complexities by occasionally striking a conveniently placed cymbal with one of his feet. The music was both rhythmic and orderly, now a waltz, now a tune in two-four time, never faster or slower. The breaks did not occur between dances but in the middle of each dance for a few brief seconds while the patronne collected a sou from each dancer, after which the dance proceeded.

The musician wore a black cloth around his throat, a black shirt, and black velours trousers. His hair was parted in the middle over his inexpressive white face with its half-closed encircled eyes, and its unnaturally red lips. Only twice while we remained did he smile, once flittingly when I sent word to him by the waiter to order a consommation and once, more lingeringly, when we departed. On these occasions the effect was almost staggering, so immobile was the ordinary cast of his features. A strange lad, a cool, cunning boy of eighteen, shredded with cocaine and absinthe, playing the accordion, monotonous in his virtuosity. He was playing when we arrived and he continued to play as we left. I like to think of him always sitting there passively, playing the accordion and shaking his sleighbells. He suggested something that would always be there, but I know it is not so, for even the next summer he had disappeared along with the bal and now he may have been shot in the Battle of the Marne or he may have strangled his girl and been transported to Devil's Island.

As for the dancers, they proved to be honest working people of the quarter. The phrase, " mal frequenté," it appeared, referred to social distinctions. The women wore loose blouses, tucked in plaid skirts, or dark blue skirts, or multi-coloured calico skirts. If you have seen the lithographs of Steinlen you can reconstruct the picture with no difficulty. The men wore espadrilles, huge pantaloons of blue velours or canvas, and bright coloured shirts with red or black sashes. The couples danced in that peculiar fashion so much in vogue in the northern outlying districts of Paris. The men seized the women tightly and the pairs whirled to the inexorable rhythm when it was a waltz, until I remembered how the Viennese become dervishes and Japanese mice when they hear Johann Strauss. In the dances in two-four time, their dances more resembled ours, something between a one-step, a mattchiche and a tango, with fascinating intermediate steps of their own devising, the whole in an utterly folkdance manner. Yes, under their experienced treading, the dance became a real dance of the people and when we entered into it, although we tried to follow their example, our feet seemed heavy and our steps conventional. How they laughed at us! The musician emphasized the effect of folkdancing by playing old songs of France which he mingled with his repertory of café-concert airs.

This was my first night at a bal musette and my last that year, for shortly afterwards I left for Italy and in Italy one does not dance. The next season found me ready to renew the adventure, to again enjoy the simple pleasures of the bal musette. I have said I was perhaps in error in recalling the street as the Rue Jessaint. Perhaps I was right and the old house had disappeared. At any rate, when I searched I could not find the bal, not even a bar. So again I appealed for help, this time to a chauffeur who appeared to understand immediately what I required, but he drove me rapidly to the district near the Halles. I was beginning to believe that after all the man had misunderstood me or was stupid. He will take me to a cabaret, l'Ange Gabriel or . . . I thought to myself as I considered the reputation of this dive where the apaches come to the surface to feel the purse of the tourist, who buys drinks as he listens to stories of murders, some of which have been committed, for it is true that the real apaches go there. I know, because my friend Fernand told me it was in l'Ange Gabriel that he had knocked all the teeth down the throat of his Angélique. (You may find the lives of these fantastic souteneurs vividly and amusingly described in that amazing book of Charles-Henry Hirsch, Le Tigre et Coquelicot. It is the only book I have read about these creatures of modern Paris that is worth its pages.[1]) However, the idea of l'Ange Gabriel was not amusing to me this evening and I leaned forward to demand of my chauffeur if he had it in mind to substitute another attraction for a bal musette. His reply was reassuring. It took the form of a gesture, the waving of a hand towards a small lighted globe depending over the doorway of an obscure marchand de vin. On this globe was painted in black letters the single word bal. We were in the narrow Rue des Gravilliers, and the bal was the Bal des Gravilliers.[2]

The bar, which one enters, is so small that one has no intimation of the really splendid aspect of the dancing-room, actually two rooms, separated by the dancing floor, two rooms ranged with long tables with long wooden benches between them. Benches also line the white walls.

---

[1] It is only fair to state that I read Carco much later. Jésus-le-Caille is, of course, the best novel dealing with this milieu.

[2] Still later aspects of the bal musette are now to be observed in the Rue de Lappe.

The lighting is brilliant. The musicians play in a little balcony below the blue-grey frieze and here there are two of them, an accordionist and a guitarist. The performer on the accordion is a virtuoso. He takes delight in winding florid ornament around the melodies he plays, after the manner of some brilliant singer impersonating Rosina in Il Barbiere. As in the Rue Jessaint a sou is demanded in the middle of each dance, but there the likeness between the two places ceases, for the life here is both gayer and more ominously evil.

A short woman enters. " Elle s'avance en se balançant sur ses hanches comme une pouliche du haras de Cordoue ": she suggests an operatic Carmen in her swagger. She is slender with dark, cropped hair worn like that of a mediæval page in the frescoes of Gozzoli, and she flourishes a cigarette, the smoke from which wreathes upward and obscures, or at any rate makes more vaguely subtle, the poignancy of her deep blue eyes and softens the snubness of her nose. It is the môme Estelle, and as she passes down the narrow aisle there is a stir of excitement at the tables. The men raise their eyes. Edouard le petit flicks a louis carelessly between his thumb and forefinger with the long dirty nails and then carries it back to his pocket. Do not mistake the gesture. It is not made to entice the girl, nor is it a sign of affluence. It is Edouard's means of demanding another louis before the night is up, if it be only a louis de dix francs. Estelle boldly returns his glance.

AU BAL MUSETTE

There is no fear in her eyes. The music is playing and Estelle dances with Carmella, l'Arabe. Edouard glowers and pulls his grey cap lower over his eyes. Suddenly he is on the floor and Estelle is pressed close to his body, still waltzing. Carmella in turn soon is dancing with another fellow. Estelle and Edouard are now whirling, whirling, and all the while his dark eyes look down piercingly into her blue eyes. The music stops. Estelle fumbles in her stocking for two sous. Edouard lights a Maryland.

Estelle smiles. Her lips move and she speaks quickly to Edouard le petit. He does not listen. Why should he listen to her? She is wasting her time here anyway. He becomes impatient for her to go on the street. In a brief second of chance Carmella, across the room, answers Estelle's smile, holding up three fingers — it is now one-thirty. Estelle quickly nods an affirmation. The musicians are always playing except in the middle of the dance when the patronne, a huge, red-faced woman with straw-colour hair, gathers in the sous. Only from one young man of twenty, her dancing partner, she takes nothing. Between dances with him she pays for his drinks. Estelle slowly walks out, Carmella, l'Arabe, following her with her eyes. Edouard le petit lights a Maryland and poises a louis between his thumb and forefinger, the nails of which are long and dirty.

November 11, 1915.

HOW MR. GEORGE MOORE RESCUED
A LADY FROM EMBARRASSMENT

HOW MR. GEORGE MOORE RESCUED
A LADY FROM EMBARRASSMENT

What the editors want nowadays is indelicate stories, told with delicacy, Mr. George Moore was saying to me. He was about to relate the history of Euphorian in Texas in so far as it involved its contingent publication in American periodicals, but he had awakened in me a chain of memories which led me back through his books. There was The Confessions of a Young Man, which apparently shocked the British matron when it appeared, and yet now Mr. Moore admits, I did not know how to write confessions when I wrote that book. I was cautiously feeling my way with the public. After I had read Jean-Jacques Rousseau's Confessions my eyes were opened. . . . Readers of the Memoirs of My Dead Life will remember how the Messrs. Appleton mutilated the work for America by " simply taking parts out of " The Lovers of Orelay and In the Luxembourg Gardens. The editors of the Tauchnitz library avoided the difficulty in a less subtle but far more humane manner: in their edition of the book they omitted the two dangerous stories. As a consequence of this gratuitous advertising the adventures of Doris and Mr. Moore at Orelay and Mildred's confession in the Luxembourg

Gardens naturally have been much discussed, but for me, the pages devoted to Marie Pellegrin and the account of Ninon's Table d'Hôte are finer art. By the time we come to Hail and Farewell we discover that Mr. Moore has acquired the ultimate technique of confessing, but few of the pages in this trilogy deal with indelicate subjects. May it not be said, indeed, that the heroine of the three sturdy volumes is Lady Gregory, who long ago published her inconsiderate opinion of Mr. Moore when she asked Sir Edwin Arnold in the Irish author's presence to inscribe his name on one of the sticks of a fan on which she was collecting autographs? Perhaps because she had read his poems, of one volume of which he was himself so ashamed that he had torn out the title page from every copy he could lay his hands on, she did not ask Mr. Moore for his autograph, although at that time he had already written A Modern Lover and The Confessions of a Young Man. When Mr. Moore relates this incident in Vale, we immediately question ourselves, Is not Lady Gregory covered with confusion for having collected autographs on fan sticks? and then, Who is Sir Edwin Arnold?

There is, of course, the episode of the cat in Salve, but that, certainly is not delicately told. This is one of Mr. Moore's Rabelaisian moods. Moreover, there is some chatter about women here and there, la belle Hollandaise, the tale of Alice and Lewis. It is in his account of Alice and Lewis that Mr. Moore took his revenge on the petty tyrannies of his American publisher. Where was the executioner with his blue pencil, the gentleman who had "simply taken parts out of" the Memoirs, when that awful phrase got into Lewis's mouth? Mr. Moore himself told me that it was an experiment, and he was as much astonished as any one to see it in print, in both the English and American editions, even in Tauchnitz. . . . One of the most powerful literary aphrodisiacs ever written, Mr. Moore says somewhere of Evelyn Innes. Spring Days is (or was) strong meat and A Drama in Muslin has a gamey flavour. I have James Huneker's copy of this book, plentifully inscribed on the margins with comments of which "Sapphic, Lesbian love," and "Lock her up — she's a woman lover!" [1] are two mild examples. Analogous libidinous passages occur in A Mummer's Wife, Esther Waters, and Euphorian in Texas.

Mr. Moore regards the American editor as a tyrant. The editor of the Century Magazine once besought him for a paper. I remembered, Mr. Moore explained to me, a lecture on Shakespeare and Balzac which I had delivered in French and I offered to translate this for the Century. This task caused me an enormous amount of trouble and I shall never do such a thing again. I found myself my own worst translator. This, however, was by no means the end

---

[1] What comments, one is forced to wonder, would Mr. Huneker find suitable to inscribe on the margins of Painted Veils?

of my embarrassments, for the editor now asked me to metamorphose my lecture into an essay. Why transform a good lecture into a bad essay? I asked myself. Days passed by, even months, but the Century did not publish my lecture and, at length, I convinced myself that as it was paid for I might yield to this editor's foolish desire and so I wrote him that I would do as he wished. Sometimes when you give a man his way, he will give you yours, and it was so on this occasion, but when the lecture was published, the final paragraph had been deleted, and this deletion resulted in my receiving a letter of apology from the editor, who was really very nice. In the last paragraph, it seemed, I had referred to the French language as my mistress, with whom I had long had a liaison, but I am not even permitted to have a liaison with a language in America. . . .

What the editors want nowadays is indelicate stories, told with delicacy, said Mr. Moore. So I wrote Euphorian in Texas for the Smart Set. What a vulgar name for a magazine! The editors kept it for a time and then they had a change of heart and made a new profession of faith: no more stories of this character were to appear in the Smart Set and Euphorian was returned to me, a most impertinent procedure, but it will be published in the July number of the English Review which should be out tomorrow.

As I had never read Goethe's Faust, this title suggested

nothing to me, but a few weeks later in Florence I caught the name shining from a book by Vernon Lee on a shelf at the Villa Allegra, and opening to the first page I read: Euphorian is the name given by Goethe to the marvellous child born of the mystic marriage of Faust and Helen. Mr. Moore's story relates how Honor came from Texas to conceive a child in England which should give a literature to her native state. Why, asks Mr. Moore plaintively, did she make application to me rather than to Meredith, Swinburne, Yeats, Henry James, or Gosse? Whatever the reason, led on by some quality in his books, she had chosen him and had not found him personally displeasing, and so we have the story of how Texas literature was created, if it ever is created, and Mr. Moore said to me, not without vanity, I am the father of Texas literature.

I remember buying the English Review on a very hot summer day from a newsstand in a station of the London tube. Fania Marinoff and I had been visiting the Billingsgate Market, following a sudden and irrepressible inspiration to spend a morning as uncomfortably as possible. We had watched a cockney miss chopping the heads from live eels and carving the wriggling lengths into small pieces. Won't they bite you? was Fania's query. Not if you looks out for 'em, replied the girl and she showed signs of expertness. At a brewery hard by lager beer was brewing and Fania stood treat at the tap to perhaps fifty women, many with children at breast. There were four in the beginning, but the news spread and if we had stayed a little longer all Shoreditch and Whitechapel would have arrived. We bought the English Review in the tube station and I began to read Euphorian aloud, but the tube was too hot and too noisy; so we got out at the Tower and took a bus. We proposed to lunch at Pagani's in Great Portland Street and we should have descended at the junction of Oxford and Regent Streets, but reading Euphorian on top of a London bus in the broiling sunglare was such a delightful pastime that we were well up Oxford Street before we realized that we must have gone too far.

Perhaps Mr. Moore has not published all his stories, but he has related most of them and one he told me last summer will bear retelling. A picture is the pivot of this tale and it will be remembered that pictures often form the basis for Mr. Moore's delightful entertaining. Come to see my pictures, he had invited me in Paris the summer before and he held Fania Marinoff breathless as he dilated on the astonishing whiteness of the breasts of Manet's women. In Euphorian stands the phrase: I followed her thinking that Monet's flooded meadows with willows rising out of the mist would help us to get over the first five minutes.

The story I am about to relate was told to me by Mr. Moore in reply to a remark of mine concerning one of his portraits which hangs on the wall of the dining-room (which is also the sitting-room) of his house in Ebury Street. I dislike being photographed, he explained, and so

66

when I am asked for my portrait I usually send a photograph of that painting, but it isn't very good. It was never completed. The artist worked very slowly and when one day I asked her how Marshall Ney had died and she replied, I believe he was executed, bursting into tears, I could bear it no longer. I never went back.

I had happened to notice a picture of hers at an exhibition in Dublin when I was writing art criticism for the Irish Times. She was a pre-Raphaelite painter and rather a good one. Liking her picture, I had praised it and, a little later, meeting me at a reception, she thanked me. But, my dear woman, I expostulated, you must be mistaken. I have never praised your picture. Yes, you have, she said, recalling the article to my mind. I had forgotten both the picture and her name. It was on this occasion that she asked me to pose for her.

The portrait was never finished. The hands are too small. She had promised to make them larger. But even unfinished, it is better than that one, and he pointed to a small painting of himself sitting in a chair, a painting which hung near the window in a bad light and which consequently could only be examined if one were very close to it.

There is an amusing story connected with that picture. Not long ago a lady wrote to remind me that I had promised to pose for her and asked for an appointment so that we might discuss the matter. I could not recall that I had

ever promised to do anything of the sort but, not wishing
to be rude, I answered her letter, suggesting an hour when
it would be convenient for me to see her. She came and
I was told she was waiting in the sitting-room. The moment I entered she blurted out her story. She was not an
artist. I had not promised to pose for her. She desired
my acquaintance and she had employed this method of
acquiring it. After this confession, she succumbed to embarrassment, lapsing into an appalling silence. During the
whole of an horrible hour I attempted to restore her, but
she was hopelessly abashed; she could not even summon up
the courage to depart. Not one syllable could she utter,
although I broached subject after subject in a vain effort
to draw her out. In desperation, I requested her to look
at that picture in the corner by the window. Then, as she
bent over to examine it, her back turned, with one knee
on a chair sustaining her, I gave her a slight pinch in the
buttocks. . . . Mr. Moore playfully imitated the gesture. . . . She turned, flushed and startled. Why did
you do that? she demanded. I do wish you hadn't done
that, and she went to the table to draw on her long gloves.
My dear lady, I said, I've tried in every way to arouse you,
to put you at your ease, and without success. At last
perhaps I have succeeded. . . . It was true. Really a
clever woman, she put her hands to her face and burst
into a fit of uncontrollable laughter. Now we were friends.
She motored with me to the French consulate, where I had

an engagement, waited for me outside, and afterwards I took her to her home in Chelsea, and she promised to come to see me again. . . .

Mr. Moore paused. After a little while he continued: It was an extraordinary incident and it would go well into a novel, but it would be difficult to give it the proper tone, to exclude vulgarity. There was nothing vulgar about it . . . I don't think, he added, that I could write it.

I will try, I announced modestly.

November, 1914

AN INTERRUPTED CONVERSATION

AN INTERRUPTED CONVERSATION

Ordinarily one does not learn facts about onself from Edmund Gosse, but my discovery that I am a Pyrrhonist is due to that literary man. A Pyrrhonist, Mr. Gosse has written, is one who doubts whether it is worth while to struggle against the trend of things. The man who continues to cross the road leisurely, although the cyclists' bells are ringing, is a Pyrrhonist — and in a very special sense, for the ancient philosopher who gives his name to the class made himself conspicuous by refusing to get out of the way of careering chariots.

Now the most unfamiliar friend I have ever walked with knows my extreme impassiveness at the corners of streets, remembers the careless manner with which I saunter from kerb to kerb, whether it be across the Grands Boulevards, Piccadilly, or Fifth Avenue. Only once[1] has this nonchalant defiance of traffic caused me to come to even temporary grief; that was on the last night of the year 1913 when, in attempting to cross Broadway, I was upset, top hat and all, by a swiftly moving vehicle, which

[1] I am unfortunately obliged to report that since this paper was written and published I have again been knocked down by an automobile, this time with more serious results.

73

passed completely over me before I was aware of what had actually happened. Then a policeman, book and pencil in hand, was stooping over me and another holding the victorious taxi-cab at bay some yards further up the street. I was not hurt and I waved them away with a magnanimous gesture.

I owe many interesting encounters to my very carelessness in this respect. It is thus that, one August day in Paris, I ran plump into Mark Colfax, an American friend whom I see far too seldom.

It was one of those charming days which make August perhaps the most delightful month to spend in Paris. Many a sly French pair, bored with Deauville or Le Touquet, return surreptitiously to the Paris Boulevards in August. On this particular day almost all the winey seduction of an October day was in the air, a splendid warm-cool splendour filtering down from the sunlight through the faded chestnut leaves, leaving vivid splotches of purple and orange on the trottoirs — a really marvellous day which I was enjoying in that most excellent occupation in Paris of gazing into shops and, passing cafés, staring into the faces of those who sat on the terrasses. This, however, is an occupation for one alone, and so when I encountered Colfax we joined a terrasse ourselves. We were near the Café Napolitain and there he and I sat down to talk. He explained in the beginning that he had a mission to fulfil. He wished to renew his acquaintanceship with a girl, a little Polish beauty who had captivated his senses a day or so earlier, brought to him quite by chance in an hotel where the patron supplied his clients with such pleasure as his address book afforded. I knew the patron myself, a fluent, amusing sort of person, who had been a cuirassier and who resembled Mayol. It was his boast that he had never disappointed a customer and it is certain that he would promise anything. There were, however, those unkind enough to say that his stock in trade was one moderately pretty girl who assumed costumes, ages, hair, and accents to please whatever demand was made upon her. The Grand Duchess Anastasia, it was rumoured, had dined with Marcel once at his little hotel, and certainly one king had been known to go there, and even a member of the English royal family, but despite these signs of social favour, Marcel continued to remain simple and obliging.

When will you look up the little Polonaise? I inquired, as we sipped Amer Picon and stared with fresh interest at each new boot and ankle that passed.

Why don't you come with me? Mark demanded in reply. Oh, I know that you are in no mood for pleasure, he went on impatiently. The point is that I shall have to wait. Marcel will be obliged to send for the girl. It is a bore to be alone in a room with red curtains and a picture of Cupid and Psyche on the walls. What have you been doing? . . . Paying the bill, he started to leave without attending upon my reply. It was evident that he counted on my complaisance. As a matter of fact I rose immediately and accompanied him down the boulevard.

What is there to do in Paris in August but enjoy oneself? I asked. I have made friends with a souteneur and his girl. We eat bread and cheese and drink bad red wine on the fortifications. In the afternoon I walk. Sometimes I go to the Luxembourg Gardens to hear the band bray sad music, or to watch the little boys play diavolo and sail their tiny boats across the fountain pond. Sometimes I walk quite silently up the Avenue Gabriel with its melancholy rows of trees while I dream that I am a Grand Duke. In the evening I may dine at the Auberge de Clou on the Avenue Trudaine or at the Cou-Cou. After dinner it is pleasant and even amusing to sit on the terrasse of one of the big cafés or to inspect the revue at La Cigale, but it is all determined, my day and night, by what happens and by whom I meet. . . . Have you seen Jacques Blanche's portrait of Nijinsky?

I think it is Picasso that interests me now, Mark replied. He puts wood and pieces of paper into his composition; architecture, that's what it is. I don't go to Blanche's any more. The atmosphere is too perfect there. The books are by all the famous writers and they are all dedicated to Blanche. The pictures are of all the great men of today and they are all painted by Blanche. . . .

I met the Countess of Jena there the other day, I responded. She had scarcely left the room before three persons volunteered, senza rancora, to tell her story. She is a devout Catholic and her husband contrived in some way to substitute a spy for the priest in the confessional. He acquired an infinite amount of information, but it didn't do him any good. She is so witty that every one invites her everywhere in spite of her reputation, or perhaps because of it, while he is left to dine alone at the Meurice.

It was at Blanche's last year that I met George Moore, I continued. I have just seen him again in London. He is at work on that old sketch of his, The Apostle, making a novel of it, to be called The Brook Kerith. It was originally, you may remember, the scenario for a play and for a time he thought he would complete the play because a novel meant a trip to Palestine and a journey was distasteful to him, but he finally decided to make it a novel. So he went to Palestine and remained six weeks, long enough for him to find a monastery and to study the lay of the country, for, as he explained to me, truly enough, one cannot imagine an actual landscape. One does not know whether there is a low or high horizon. There may be a river which all the characters must cross. It is necessary to see these things. Above all, he felt the necessity of finding a monastery. He described to me his thrill when he discovered an order of monks living on a narrow ledge of cliff with five hundred feet sheer rise and descent above and below it. Now his work was done and he returned to England to write the book, a reaction from the work of his immediate past, for he told me he was tired of being personal in literature. The book will exhibit a conflict between two types: Christ, the disappointed mystic who recognizes the fact that no good will be served in saving the world by his death, and Paul, full of hope, idealism, and illusions. It is the drama of the conflict between the nature which is affected by externals and that which is not, he told me.

It is a subject for Anatole France, Mark retorted. Moore, in my opinion, is not a novelist. His great achievements are his memoirs. I was interested in Evelyn Innes and Esther Waters, but I felt that something vital was lacking. There is nothing lacking in the three volumes of Hail and Farewell. They grow in interest. Moore has found his métier.

But he insists, I explained before the door of the little hotel which was our destination, that Hail and Farewell is a novel. He becomes infuriated when some one suggests that it is a book after the manner, say, of The Reminiscences of Lady Randolph Churchill.

Entering, we walked up one flight of stairs.

Do you mean the incidents are untrue? Mark demanded.

Before the concierge's door stood Marcel, his white apron spread neatly over his ample paunch. It was early in the afternoon and the room beyond, usually occupied by girls waiting to be selected, was empty.

Ah, monsieur est revenu! Marcel exclaimed in his piping voice, as he ushered us into the very chamber with the red curtains and the painting of Cupid and Psyche that Mark had described. C'est pour la petite Polonaise sans doute que monsieur revient?

Oui, Mark answered. Faut-il attendre longtemps?

Mais non, monsieur, un petit moment. Elle habite en face. Je vais envoyer le garçon la chercher tout de suite. Et pour monsieur, votre ami?

Je ne desire rien, I said.

Marcel bowed with mock humility. Comme monsieur voudrait. Then a doubt appeared to assail him. Peut-être que la petite Polonaise suffira à tous les deux?

Jamais de la vie! I shouted. Flûte, Mercure, allez! Je suis puceau!

Marcel was equal to this. Et ta sœur? he demanded as he disappeared down the stairs.

I lounged on the bed while Mark sat on a chair and smoked.

No, I replied, they are true, but it is ordered and selected, even stylized truth.

I am beginning to understand. Other memoirs, as a rule, have neither selection nor form and are not altogether accurate in the bargain. . . .

Exactly, I said. Moore says there are those who insist that Balzac was greater than Turgeniev because the Frenchman drew his characters from his imagination, the Russian his from life. You may recall, however, that Edgar Saltus once remarked: The manufacture of fiction from facts was begun by Balzac. Moore's point is that all great writers write from observation. There is no other way. A character may bear more or less resemblance to the model which inspired it. The name may be changed, the derivation may be extremely remote: still some resemblance remains. In a letter which Moore once wrote me stands the phrase: Memory is the mother of the Muses, a perfectly literal statement of fact, for Melpomene, Thalia, and their seven sisters were actually the daughters of Mnemosyne. According to Moore then, Hail and Farewell is just as much a work of imagination as A Nest of Noblemen or Les Illusions Perdues.

It is true, admitted Mark, that many a writer has suffered through the recognition of some character or other. Dickens was often in trouble. Oscar Wilde is said to have done himself in Dorian Gray and Meredith's models for The Tragic Comedians and Diana of the Crossways are well known.

While Moore has called his characters by his real names and has reported their conversations as he recalled them, you must remember, I urged Mark, that he has not reported *all* their conversations, nor has he included in the book all the people he knew at this period. Arthur Symons, for instance, a great friend of Moore at that time, is scarcely mentioned, and with reason. He played no part in the form of the book. Its plot is not concerned with him.

All artists, I continued, create only in the image of

things they have seen, translated, through their imagination, into the formal terms of art. The paintings of Mina Loy seem to the beholder the strange creations of a vagrant fancy. In one of her pictures an exquisite Indian girl stands poised before an oriental palace, the most fantastic of oriental palaces, it would seem, but the artist explained to me that it was simply the façade of Hagenbeck's menagerie in Hamburg, seen with an imaginative eye, while the girl was a paid model. One day on the beach at the Lido Mina Loy observed a young man in a bathing suit stretched on the sand with his head in the lap of a beautiful woman. Other women surrounded the two. The group immediately suggested a composition to her and she went home to paint. Removing the young man's bathing suit, she gave him wings, while she dressed the women in lovely floating robes.[1]

And once I asked Frank Harris to explain to me the origin of his vivid story, Montes the Matador. It's very simple, he replied. The model for Montes was a little greaser whom I met in Kansas. He was one of many in charge of cattle shipped up from Mexico and down from the States. All the white cattle men, the gringos, held him in great contempt, as was their way with greasers, but, continued Harris, speaking deliberately with his beautifully modulated voice, his eyes twinkling with the memory

[1] The painting, which is called l'Amour dorloté par les belles dames, now hangs in my drawing-room.

of the incident, I soon discovered that the greaser's contempt for the gringos was immeasurably greater than theirs for him. Bah, he would say to me, they know nothing. And it was so. He could go into a cattle car on a pitch black night and make the bulls stand up, a feat that none of the white men would have attempted. I asked him how he did this and he replied, I know them. He could go into a herd of cattle just let loose together and pick out their leader immediately, pick him out before the cattle themselves had! He was really the origin of Montes the Matador. The character was named, of course, after the famous torero described by Gautier in his Voyage en Espagne. When I went to Madrid some years later I attended a number of bull-fights before I put the story together. But, I asked Harris, is it possible for an espada to stand in the bull-ring with his back to the bull, during a charge, as you have made him do frequently in the story? Of course not, he answered me at once, smiling his frankly malevolent smile. Of course not. That part was put in to show how much the public will stand for in a work of fiction. I believe a torero tried it some time after the book appeared and was killed instantly.

Fiction, history, poetry, criticism, at their best are all the same thing. When they inflame the imagination and stir the pulse they are in one sense identical: all creative work. It does not matter what a man writes about. It matters how he writes it. Subject is nothing. Should we regard

AN INTERRUPTED CONVERSATION

Velázquez as less important than Murillo because he painted portraits of his contemporaries, whom in his fashion he criticized, while Murillo disguised his models in the robes of the Virgin? Walter Pater's description of the Monna Lisa would live if the picture disappeared. Indeed, it has created a factitious interest in da Vinci's La Gioconda. Even more might be said for Huysmans's description of Moreau's Salomé which actually puts the figures in the picture in motion! The critic, the historian, at their best are creative artists as writers of fiction are creative artists. Should we regard Imperial Purple less a work of creative art than Silas Lapham?

I am getting your meaning more and more, said Mark, and it occurs to me that perhaps I have been unjust in rating Moore low as a novelist. Perhaps I should have said that he is more successful in those books which depend more on his memory and less on his imagination. He cannot, after all, he added, have known Jesus and Paul. . . .

You are quite wrong, I replied, at least from his point of view. He says he knows Paul better than he has ever known any one else. He even finds hair on Paul's chest. He can describe Paul, I believe, to the last mole. He knows his favourite colours, and whether he preferred artichokes to alligator pears. As for Christ, everybody professes to know Christ these days. Since the world has become definitely anti-Christian it has become comparatively simple to discuss the Saviour. He is regarded as an historical character and a much more human one than Napoleon. I have heard anarchists in bar-rooms talk about him by the hour, sometimes very graphically and always with a certain amount of wit. I assure you, it is all the same. Now that he has been to Palestine and read the Gospels for the first time, Moore feels as well acquainted with Christ and Paul as he does with Edward Martyn and Lady Gregory.

I must fall back on the personal then, Mark said, now really at bay, and state that I am less moved when Moore is describing Evelyn Innes than when he tells of his affair with Doris at Orelay.

I am glad you mentioned Evelyn Innes again, I replied, because it is in this very book that he is said to have painted so many of his friends. Yeats undoubtedly sat for the portrait of Ulick Dean while it has been suggested that Arnold Dolmetsch posed for the picture of Evelyn's father. Dolmetsch's testimony on this point goes farther. He says that he dictated certain passages in the book. . . .

What is it then? What is the difference? There is some difference. Of that I am sure.

The difference is —I began, when the door opened and Marcel entered, the most amazingly comprehensive smile on his countenance.

Mademoiselle vous attend, he announced, and he looked the question: Shall I bring her in here?

Mark answered the unuttered words immediately with,

AN INTERRUPTED CONVERSATION

Je viens, tossing to me a short, Wait, as he vanished through the doorway.

Moving to the window, I drew aside the red curtains, and looked down into the fountain-splashed court below.

    *   *   *   *   *   *   *

What is the difference?

I suppose it is that you prefer the later Moore to the earlier Moore, the author of the more recent and better written books to the author of A Mummer's Wife. Evelyn Innes was many times rewritten. Moore has said that he could never get it to suit him, but he has also said recently that he would never re-write another book, a resolution he has not kept. Memoirs of My Dead Life and Hail and Farewell do not need rewriting. They are written for posterity. The Brook Kerith, you will perhaps find equally to your taste. It will be the latest Moore. . . .

You have explained the difference, Mark said. It is one of development. Now that I think of it, I don't believe that Anatole France could write The Brook Kerith. He would be tempted to make it both symbolical and cynical. Moore, through his acquaintanceship with the characters will make it more human. I wonder, he continued musingly, fumbling in his pocket for money to pay Marcel, as we left the room and descended the stairs, if he told you whether that hair on Paul's chest was red or black . . . ?

February 1, 1915.

THE NIGHTINGALE AND
THE PEAHEN

THE NIGHTINGALE AND
THE PEAHEN

One summer day Fania Marinoff and I sat on the bat-
tlemented terrace of Windsor Castle, facing brick-built
Eton across the Thames. The atmosphere was clear and the
scene was so suggestive of old England that, very natu-
rally, one was prone to think of almost anything else, just
as, probably, the old English were. Silently we sat with
our vagrant memories until, startled by the shrill call of a
peacock, we turned to see the lawn behind us veritably
peopled with these resplendent birds. Eventually my
thoughts found utterance in the following story:

It is believed by the present owners that the Villa Allegra originally belonged to the Medici family who may
have employed it at one time as a residence for the court
physician, for it rises but little higher on the hill behind
the royal palace that one approaches by the cypress-lined
ascent of the Stradone del Poggio Imperiale. Legend has it
that Raphael designed the façade. Later the Villa passed
into other less reverent hands and it occurred to one occu-
pant to wall up the cortile and make small store-rooms
of the space. It was Leonard Dale who, in the process of his
most successful restoration of the Villa, divined this van-
dalism. Wielding an ax, he shattered the plaster walls,

exposing to view a series of graceful, slender marble columns. Dale's first startled cry was Brunelleschi! and it may well have been that artist who created the magic proportions of these columns. Leonard Dale further embellished the Villa with a salone and the lovely loggia where Eleanora Duse was wont to stand in imitation of her famous photograph in La Città Morta, gazing sadly over towards the hills of the Certosa. There is scarcely a prospect in Italy which is not pleasing to the eye, but I can recall no other view more beautiful than this. It is not easy for me to resist the desire to describe the beauty and mystery of the Villa Allegra: the sunken marble bath in which, in the morning, it was advisable to kill the scorpions before bathing, the rope ladder, coiled under a trap-door in the floor of Dale's second storey chamber ready to be let down when he wished to pay a visit to Edith's chamber beneath, the red Roman damask-covered walls of the salone, hung with Chinese paintings and faded primitive madonnas, the Persian miniatures on the yellow walls of another chamber, the antechamber to the salone, vast and perfect in its proportions, walking through which one caught a glimpse of Jacques Blanche's portrait of Edith Dale and her son, the renaissance dining-room with its outlook on the garden, and the garden itself where dinner was often served in the cool evening among the plane-trees and laurels, the gardenias and the crape-myrtles, dinner which was frequently interrupted by the peacock.

NIGHTINGALE AND PEAHEN

Yes, there was a peacock, a magnificent bird, who strutted up and down in his enclosure at the back of the garden, shrieking to acquaint us with his woe. His grief was identical with that of the Siamese cat, whose tawny fur melted into chocolate and whose cries matched the piercing blue of his eyes. Both creatures suffered from the same complaint: both had lost their mates. The cat expressed his suffering in long-drawn wails, heart-rending, so curiously did they resemble the cries of an infant. How would Baudelaire and Gautier, those French literary lovers of cats, have alleviated the misery of the exotic beast? A new dialogue des Bêtes is suggested for Colette between a peacock and a Siamese cat, both of whom have lost their women-kind. The cat, I believe, followed his spouse into the feline Nirvana. At least there came a day when he was seen and heard no more. At one time, however, there was a trio of brooding creatures at the Villa Allegra, for the lodge-keeper's wife had lost her child daughter, who only the year before had smiled as she clung to the bars of the gate as it swung open. Now the bereaved woman's eyes leered with a kind of morbidity that caused every one for whom she opened the gate to turn away helplessly. Was it only Mina Loy who dared protest sufficiently to paint her motherhood, with the dead child at her feet, upbraiding Mary?

The peacock was caged for, of all the unhappy creatures at the Villa, he alone was dangerous. He had become, in fact, a menace to girlhood. Many a frail, white-robed child had visited the Italian garden in the soft morning or the green twilight to be met and pursued, and to flee, pale with fright, to the locked security of her chamber in the Villa. Then the bird of passion would stalk the terrace, crying angrily aloud, desperate and ashamed, for a long time afterwards, until in the end a cage was devised to confine the proud and tragic fowl. Even yet, sometimes, while the monkey in the same enclosure was being fed, the peacock escaped to render dinner in the garden a dangerous adventure for those who partook of it.

The shadow of romantic disaster persistently hung over the beautiful Villa, and some have questioned whether any living being, bird, beast, or man, would be happy there. The strange presence described as a ghost kept successive visitors tortured with doubt and terror. They could not sleep: their beds rocked, their feet were pinched, and writhing shudders possessed their souls. What an immensity of horror lies in the possibility of being choked out of one's last gasp by a bloodless, strangling, unseen hand! For an entire night one man hurled malisons at the unwelcome spectre, walking the floor while he shrieked horrid names at her, and then he fell into a delirium from which he did not recover for days. The chatelaine, now wishing to rid herself of the presence, called in a priest to exorcise her with holy water, book, and candle, and now perversely desiring her to return, invited a professor of black magic to hold incantation ceremonies in the salone, while the servants huddled in corners, making proper signs against the power of the evil eye. Certainly illness and desolation and a mighty despair spread their pall over the Villa Allegra.

There was always the sense of something beyond life in the strange green nights on the Florentine hills, in the road below which the golden-voiced peasant sang, refusing money, happy if his music reached the ears of the Signora above him. One such night a dumb curiosity seized Peter Whiffle and me and caused us to desert our chairs on the loggia where the tall bottles of golden Strega stood, half-full, and the flames of the Roman lamps flickered in the faint breeze, to seek the chamber directly above the spot where we had been sitting, the temporary abode of two white Persian cats. The room was empty when we entered it: the bright moonlight streaming in from the doorway, leading to a terrace which formed the roof of the loggia, told us that. Noiselessly, and apparently unreasonably, we stole carefully across the broad chamber and looked out. I can still recall the expression of amazement on Peter's face, perhaps reflected on my own, as we stood just hidden by the hangings at the doorway and saw the two cats softly lift their padded paws from the backs of two white doves who rose unsteadily, dizzily, and lazily into the green atmosphere, while the cats rolled on their backs, stretching their claws to the air and making faint

mews. Did we learn why the hawk and the cat sit together in the temples of the Nile?

The peacock had been brought to the Villa Allegra
from Florence with his somewhat more dully painted companion, the peahen. She had always known him and the
brilliant colours of his tail, which he had spread out before
her to capture her attention when he was courting her
and upon which he continued to rely to hold her relaxed
interest, were as faded and unthrilling a commonplace
to her as Saint Mark's Square in Venice is to a gondolier,
but, like most husbands, he was unaware of this fact.

See what a glorious bird am I! he would cry as he
strutted and posed for her. Even in the narrow enclosure in
which he had been confined in the Florentine bird-shop,
so near to the steps where the rose-coloured lotus blooms
on their long stalks were offered for sale, he had succeeded
in partially displaying the blue-green and green-blue en-
amels of his feathers.

Already, however, she knew that she was bored . . .
and she had not yet heard singing, but one night, as the
two were strutting on the wall which separated the terrace
from the olive grove, she, in hypocritical, humble ob-
servance of the more brilliant hues in her lord's throat,
suddenly became aware of what throats were really made
for. On the instant his iridescent plumage was transformed
to a muddy black in her vision when, for the first time,
she heard the nightingale sing in the copse below. Her

heart almost stopped beating, but the peacock was unaware of her ecstasy. He continued to strut. Was he not the only peacock at the Villa Allegra?

Was it the next night that she merged her fancy in the music of the singing bird? I do not know, but soon thereafter she plunged recklessly after the love-notes that issued from the throat of the nightingale. The peacock came to his senses with a jolt, realizing immediately how greatly he needed her. Without her attention, indeed, his poses lost all their meaning. His cries now became piercing; his anguish was terrible to behold. He refused food and his strut became a swift, anxious walk which extended the entire length of the terrace and back again. This was his life for three days and three nights when, quite unexpectedly, the little peahen crept back, mostly devoid of her ferruginous feathers, a sorry, scraggy creature stripped of illusions.

Then the beautiful thing happened. The peacock caressed her pathetic throat, he preened her feathers, and, as a final proof of his forgiving nature, he strutted the terrace and displayed before her the glory of his tail. No mere peahen could have withstood these gallant attentions. He again became her lord and she was faithful to him until she died.

One green moonlight night on the terrace of the Villa Allegra, Lili de Luxembourg, who had loved so often and so much, spoke to me about nightingales.

SACRED AND PROFANE MEMORIES

You can hear them quite near Paris, she was saying, and how beautifully they sing! Their trill especially is wonderful. Their music is so lusty when they are in love that towards the end of the summer their voices become worn like the voices of old tenors.

January 7, 1915.

JULY–AUGUST 1914

JULY–AUGUST 1914

I

Wednesday, July 29

Before Madame Caillaux was acquitted rumours of war were circulating in the Paris journals, rumours which became more ominous as they were repeated by word of mouth. At the time I did not happen to be reading the papers and I first heard the news from the lips of a stranger sitting at an adjacent table on the terrasse of the Café de la Paix. There will be a big European war, this fellow announced. Austria is sure to declare war on Serbia because Serbia has not yet punished the assassin of the Archduke Ferdinand. Russia is compelled by treaty to stand by Serbia; France and England are allies of Russia; while Germany and Italy are pledged to assist Austria. This stranger exhibited a passport [1] and an American flag, both of which he expected to find useful in the event of a crisis.

Nevertheless, in the beginning I do not believe I gave much heed to this baleful declaration. It was not the first time, certainly, that war had been impending. Day by day,

[1] It was before the days when passports were demanded of casual European travellers and the exhibition was therefore impressive.

however, the situation became more serious. Eventually it became increasingly difficult to disregard the facts. There was talk of closing the Bourse in Vienna; stocks were going to smash; Austrian troops were being mobilized from the four quarters of the globe. Gold was scarce in Paris. At the American Express Company the clerk would give me only one twenty franc piece in gold out of every one hundred francs that I drew, the rest of the sum being doled out to me in silver and copper.[1] I recall that I carried about quantities of silver at this time, perhaps as many as six or eight heavy five franc silver pieces and twenty or so one franc pieces. Revolutionary demonstrations on a small scale occurred. Socialists, bearing banners with inflammatory inscriptions, marched up and down the Place de la République crying monotonously, A bas la guerre! These were put to flight, not without difficulty, by the Garde Républicaine which, in more peaceful hours, marched threateningly up and down the Grands Boulevards. Proprietors of cafés were required to remove all tables from the sidewalks. This order, however, was executed piecemeal. I observed one day that two rows of tables and chairs had been removed from the terrasse of the Café de la Paix. Next day a third row was gone. This phenomenon struck me as strange, but I do not seem to have inquired the reason for it until all the tables were taken in, when I was informed

[1] French notes in small denominations did not then exist.

that the police were convinced that these chairs on the sidewalk offered too excellent an opportunity for the congregation of radical groups.

I had been waiting in Paris for the arrival from America of Edith Dale, with whom I had been invited to spend the month of August in Florence. She had telegraphed me, indeed, from Naples the intelligence that she was coming directly to Paris to meet me, but on this very morning of July 29 I received a second telegram from her which read: Come to Florence detained. That day I happened to be lunching with Philip Moeller at the Café Napolitain. I'm afraid I made a distrait guest. I couldn't decide what to do. A little later I asked the advice of Savage at the American Express Company and he said he saw no harm in going to Italy, but he thought there would be war. At the ticket bureau the man behind the window informed me that the trains via Turin, the direct route between Italy and France, had been discontinued. One could still travel by way of the Simplon Tunnel, to be sure, but he could give no assurance that this would be permanently possible. The implications of this casual information were sufficiently devastating to keep me walking back and forth in the offices of the American Express Company on the Rue Scribe, in an endeavour to reach a decision. It was in this mood that I encountered Kate Rolla, who had just moved all her household effects to France, intending to make her future home there. Somewhat dismayed by the outlook, she was still able to smile. Perhaps it was her smile that determined me to buy a railroad ticket for Florence. After I had bought my ticket, Philip Moeller proposed a drive and, as we were driving up the Champs Elysées into the Bois, I realized that what I really wanted to do was to go back to America to see Fania Marinoff.

I was invited to dine that evening in Enghien with M. H. Hanson and I attempted to keep the appointment although the idea did not fit in very well with my present temper. The vague arrangement had been that Hanson should meet me on the platform of the Enghien railway station. As he did not do so, after I had waited perhaps ten minutes, I drove to the Casino and asked for Monsieur de Paty, the director. Yes, he replied to my query, he was expecting Mr. Hanson. Monsieur de Paty, a trifle nervous on this occasion, did not make me feel at home, although he was not lacking in a certain formal cordiality. La Traviata was announced to be performed at the Opéra of the Casino that evening and he was occupied in making reservations for some of his clients. I recalled that some one had told me that my old friend Polaire lost quantities of money gambling at Enghien. I inquired of Monsieur de Paty if she were here this evening. He replied that she had entered the gambling-rooms not half an hour earlier. Would I care to buy a ticket and join her? I refused, bearing in mind the fact that a woman when she is gambling is in no proper mood for conversation. Even a salutation becomes irksome under these conditions.

Presently Monsieur de Paty, having completed his distribution of tickets, requested me to sit with him in the café of this little Casino. Through an open doorway one caught glimpses of the gamblers as they came out of, or went into, the salle de jeu, one by one, two by two, mostly women, with serious faces — no one was smiling — cocottes or femmes du monde, almost all smartly dressed in black or white, with capes [1] on their shoulders, for it was a cool evening. Many of the ladies going in were occupied in arranging notes in their gold meshbags,[1] but it was to be observed that those coming out were not counting their money.

It was now about eight-thirty. I drank an Amer Picon Grenadine, while Monsieur de Paty sipped a quart de Vittel. After a time he spoke quite casually about the possibility of war. Naturally, he admitted, the situation is extremely serious, and he told me that the sous-préfet of Enghien had received his orders for mobilization the night before. Tired in mind and body, hungry and annoyed at being kept waiting for dinner, exhausted by my long siege of indecision in the afternoon, I upset my empty glass as I rose from the table and it shattered on the marble floor. Hastily bidding farewell to Monsieur de Paty, I caught a cab to the station and a train to Paris.

[1] It is an ironical fact that capes and gold meshbags are again fashionable in 1931.

Back in Paris I listlessly ordered dinner at the Petit Riche, but I found I was no longer hungry, no longer in a mood for eating. The Boulevards attracted me, the crowded Boulevards, which somehow seemed unfamiliar now that the tables and chairs had been removed from the terrasses. I strolled until I stood before Parisiana, at this epoch a cinema house, which I entered. Standing at the back, I witnessed the unreeling of one picture — it was now about ten-thirty — La Consciènce de Chauffeur, an extremely silly American film in which a little girl was shown climbing into an empty freight-car to play. She fell asleep, the brakeman unwittingly closed the door upon her, and the car rolled away with the rest of the train. The child awakened in terror and closeups of her emotions were thrown on the screen. Later she was discovered and returned to her anxious parents. After it was over the audience laughed heartily.

When I went out of the theatre, it was raining. The Garde Républicaine, the capes of the men slung over their shoulders, marched past me. I took a cab to my hotel in the Rue de Trévise and went to bed.

Thursday, July 30

The next morning I departed for Florence. With no faint notion that I should not be coming back to Paris, I left a trunk and a hat-box with the American Express Company and a Venetian vase and a pottery bowl at my hotel. Explaining that they were fragile, I promised to return for them.[1]

I bade the patronne good-bye and the taxi rolled lazily towards the Gare de Lyon. The train was scheduled to depart at eight-twenty-five and I had left the hotel in good time so that I might secure a place. At the gare, however, there was no sign of a porter and I was obliged to carry my heavy suitcase, my Italian army cape, two walking sticks, and a book almost to the train before any one offered to assist me. Just as I was entering the gate which led to the tracks a lone porter agreed to help me and eventually found me a place, the last, in a compartment on the train. Presently people were standing in this compartment and it remained disagreeably crowded most of the day. It was evident that many persons were leaving Paris for one reason or another.

The details of this journey do not remain very clear in my mind. I recall that I bought and read the morning papers. Then I read Oscar Wilde and Myself, by Lord Alfred Douglas, which I had brought with me. At some station — it may have been Pontarlier — I bought Charles Derennes's Nique et ses Cousines, which subsequently failed to amuse me. There was no one to converse with.

---

[1] It was many months before I saw these articles again and, improperly packed for shipping as they were, when I opened the packages containing the vase and the bowl in New York, it was to discover them shattered.

Because it was raining, the windows were closed a great deal of the time and, as a consequence, it was very hot. A pompous Frenchwoman, whose handkerchief carried a crest, got on with her son at Dijon and rode to Lausanne. There was another charming, little, old French lady, designated mademoiselle, with a dog and a maid, whose destination was also Lausanne. Never shall I forget this charming old lady's cry of delight, like an exultant stage-cry of Ellen Terry's in a similar situation, her nudges of joy in the side of the maid, as Lausanne appeared through the windows.

In all the French stations there were soldiers on guard, a menace of soldiers. It's the only way to clear the atmosphere, Savage had said in Paris, a big war. There is no other way. We have been expecting it for a long time and it might as well come. There was, of course, some talk about the war in the compartment, but that was quickly forgotten in the gossip of the countryside.

Somewhere in Switzerland an Italian and a Frenchman got on the train together. The Frenchman, perhaps a chauffeur, a fussy fellow, descended at Domodossola. The Italian travelled on to Milan. After the Frenchman was gone, the Italian began to ask me questions about America. Could he make money there? I assured him that *I* couldn't.

Mais vous êtes déjà riche.

Au contraire, je n'ai pas un sou. (At the moment all the money I had in the world was one hundred francs.)

Mais vous voyagez. . . .

C'est pour l'argent que je voyage.

Quel article est-ce que vous vendez?

Je ne suis pas marchand. Je suis écrivain.

Journaliste alors! Quelle chance!

When I asked him for his opinion on the possibilities of war, he volunteered, Italy will never fight on the side of Austria, in spite of the unpopular alliance made by Crispi and renewed for five years only a few months ago. We Italians detest the Austrians.

We spoke French to each other. He could not speak English. I could not speak Italian. My French was as good as his.

Late in the evening we had the compartment to ourselves. Lowering the lights, we extended ourselves the lengths of the two seats and tried to sleep. We snoozed fitfully. If it was not quite sleep, at least it was rest. The train arrived in Milan towards midnight, almost on time, and I was soon in bed at the Hotel Concordia, having left instructions to be awakened at six as the train for Florence departed at seven-ten.

II

Friday, July 31

I almost missed the train for Florence. Stopping to telegraph Edith, I only learned as I stepped away from the window that the train departed at seven and not at seven-

ten. I managed to swing on board just as she was pulling out.

A warm sun greeted my entrance into Florence, most
welcome after the cold Paris days and a good omen too, but
when I stepped out on the platform there was no one to
greet me. After all, I explained to myself, Edith has no
car. So I engaged a taxi and we started off towards the
Villa Allegra. It was just one-thirty when we drove away
in the hot sunglare. Outside the station I caught a
glimpse of Ducie Haweis in a car with a lady whose face
I did not recognize. They did not see me, so intent were
they on their projects. We drove on, down the Via Tornabuoni, across the beautiful Ponte Santa Trínita, perhaps
the most perfect of bridges, through the Porta Romana,
and up the Viale della Poggia Imperiale. The way was all
too familiar to me: I instructed the driver at every turn,
directing him past the palace with its circular marble balustrade flanked with statues, then an abrupt turn to the
left following a narrow road, until the avenue of cypresses
leading to the Villa Allegra came into view.

There was no one waiting to greet me at the door of the
Villa and so I rushed inside to find Edith sorting out
clothes in the grand salone, tossing them in and out of
trunks with a splendid energy. In a few moments she had
told me all the news. Neith Hapgood, it appeared, had
been conquered by the spectre. She had passed two nights
at the Villa, wide awake, with the lamps burning. The

third night she had slept in town and this very morning she had left with the children for Vallombrosa. It was Neith then whom I had seen in the carriage with Ducie, who had accompanied her as far as the station.

The first night, Edith said, the place got me the way it always does. I decided I would give up everything and come back here to live. I even wrote letters to my mother and Leonard about it. But I recovered from that feeling, especially when I found that Neith couldn't stay here. So now I've decided to give the place up altogether. What's the good of having it? I can't keep my friends here. I'm packing a few things, preparing to leave for ever. On Monday we join the others at Vallombrosa and I dare say I'll never come back here again. As a matter of fact the Villa is rented from October on.

In the afternoon an art critic, a friend of Edith's, arrived with a girl, who was not introduced, and his cousin and her husband, who were. Amazar was a tall, slender fellow, with a slight growth of reddish brown hair surmounting the face of an intellectual Jew. His precise mind apparently had catalogued all available human knowledge and he exploited this capacity endlessly in astonishingly brilliant conversation, tinged here and there incongruously with faint suggestions of human sympathy. It is easy to describe this conversation, but it would be difficult to reproduce its exact tone. Like many philosophers Amazar was a good deal of a dreamer. His precision of thinking did not prevent him from being unable to cope with swift changes of subject or projected alterations in his manner of living.

His companion did not make much of an impression at first as she sat hunched up, her chin supported on the palm of her hand. She was wearing tan shoes of an American make, a blue serge skirt, and over this a tunic of olive green crêpe which fell loosely half way to her knees. Thousands of women in Greenwich Village in New York were dressing like this. Presently when Edith spoke to the girl, I more closely observed her intelligent face, framed by a mass of brown hair, parted in the middle. Her laugh was hysterical and noisy, her teeth too long, her mouth unusually large. She spoke English with an accent, and occasional important lapses into French, but on the whole well. She and Edith were discussing Aleicester Crowley.

Is it true, Edith demanded, that he celebrated the Black Mass in Paris?

I do not believe it, the girl responded, but he probably celebrated masses of various kinds that people wanted. He would put himself out at any time to place some one else in a ridiculous situation. One day he told Henner Skene he wanted to learn something about music. C'était une blague. He knew a great deal about music, but it amused him to trifle with Skene's seriousness. So when Skene played Chopin for him, Crowley pretended to find it boring, but when Skene played excerpts from Cavalleria Rusticana, Crowley exclaimed: Ah, that's better! This music moves me. Skene of course protested: That's not right. You should prefer Chopin. So he played more of the Pole's music, and then again more Mascagni, and after a decent interval Crowley admitted that he was beginning to understand. The scene revolted me, the girl declared, but this was not enough for Crowley. Presently he asked Skene if he would play for a friend of his, the Princesse X. When Skene agreed, it was arranged that they should all meet in my apartment where there was a grand piano. I was certain that this would be no princess and I hated to have Skene tricked, but when he asked me if he could play for them in my apartment I could scarcely refuse. I was not present at the first audition. When they proposed to repeat the experiment, however, I determined to join them. Walking in unannounced, I discovered the " princess " in a long flowing robe curled up on the couch beside Crowley and I recognized in this woman with plaited black hair bound around her forehead, a Russian Jewish model of the quartier. While Skene played a sonata of Beethoven she and Crowley sat apparently in rapture. Their lips twitched; their eyes stared in ecstasy. Their attitude, indeed, ridiculed the performer. Furious, I was about to leave the room when suddenly in the middle of a phrase Skene stopped playing, whirling about to face us as he explained:

I can play no longer. I don't remember the rest. So the pose of Crowley and the princess was broken. It was not real any longer. *They* had now become ridiculous.

Spontaneously, she was soon talking about Herbert Rolling, an American sculptor we all knew.

I met Herbert and his wife in Paris recently. She seemed sad. I think it is saddening, you see, to live with Herbert.

She isn't much in herself, Edith put in, but she wants her own life. She wants to develop herself as far as she can and Herbert won't let her. He is too lazy to develop himself. He is talented, but he won't work.

He will never work, the girl assented. He will never do anything.

He thinks of nothing but Nietzsche now, Edith added.

It was I who taught him that, the girl assured us. At first it was Shelley. I suggested to him that he read Shelley and dutifully he bought a book of Shelley's poems and sat with it under a spreading tree in the Luxembourg Gardens. For days he could be seen sitting there with his book, but it was always the same book open at the same page. Later, it was Nietzsche. All the quartier was reading Nietzsche. It was very much the fashion. Even I was reading Nietzsche. I gave a book to Herbert and he began to believe that he was enthralled by the philosophy of Nietzsche and he was never to be seen without a copy of Beyond Good and Evil protruding from his coat pocket.

Just before he sailed, Edith said, he put that book back in his pocket. It was his last conscious gesture in America.

Indoors, a few moments later, I found an opportunity of questioning Edith. I learned that this was Lili de Luxembourg, a famous model who had been responsible for the formation of the character of more than one young American artist. She had lived with some of them: she was friends with them all. It was such a strange sight, Edith said, to see Lili in a Montparnasse café surrounded by four or five of her former lovers. Herbert Rolling, it seemed, had loved her for two years. She had now been with Amazar off and on for five years.

Edith later repeated to me what Amazar had told her. Lili, he had said, was a singer when she came to Paris, but she lost her voice. Recently she has found it again. I want to make her free, to make her independent enough to live her own life, free even to go beyond the life she has lived in the past. She is the most interesting woman I have ever known.

At dinner Lili was more or less silent. She confided to me later, perhaps in jest, that it was the first time she had ever dined in such splendour. After dinner, while Amazar talked with Edith, Lili and I strolled out to the loggia in the moonlight and I explained to her how Leonard Dale had created the new part of the Villa, including the salone and the Italian garden below us.

What luck, to be rich! Lili exclaimed, as we descended the marble steps into the garden.

Italy! I cried with the enthusiasm of youth.

I love it now, too, Lili agreed, but I didn't at first. It has taken me a long time to appreciate this country. Now, however, I find everything in France so petty in comparison.

As we left the formal garden for the terrace where the oleanders and daphnes and gardenias flourished, Lili mused aloud: There is another kind of luck, besides that of being rich. Just at the time in my life when I had reason to believe everything would be at an end, it has all begun over again. When I first went to Paris I ruined my voice by singing in the streets. So I became a model. For years I did not sing a note, but lately I have discovered that my voice is still there and I am trying to coax it back. I have an incentive to live and work for again. In the past my life was too agitated. It is more tranquil now. I am fond of Amazar. I respect him. At first, his ideas, his serious intellectual preoccupations frightened me. They do so no longer. I feel more in sympathy with life and I am less troubled with illusions. It does me good to work, to take long walks on the Italian hills. That clears the mind. One can think. The troubled past is over. I am thirty-two years old.

In the green Italian night I could not entirely reconstruct her face, but it seemed to me that it was beautiful as she sat on the low wall with her profile against the sky.

JULY–AUGUST 1914

When we went back into the Villa we found Edith and Amazar animatedly conversing in the yellow room. Our appearance was the signal for them to rise. We all went to bed at once.

Saturday, August 1

The next morning I walked down to Florence where I remained less than an hour, but I discovered I could buy no French or English newspapers of recent date, drank a cocktail at Giacosa's, dispatched Edith's telegram to John Reed in the Palazzo Nonfinito at No. 12 Via del Proconsolo, which read: Communications will be cut no mail débâcle, or words to that effect, and cashed a small draft for her at the American Express Company, but it did not occur to me to inquire about boat sailings. The principal piece of news, which I had picked up in the bookshop, was to the effect that Juarès, the French socialist leader, had been assassinated the night before in a café in Paris.

When I returned to the Villa with the information about Juarès, Edith predicted a social revolution in Paris, but Amazar reminded her that during a war the opposing factions inside a nation were likely to unite.

I have a brother in the army, said Lili. He is stationed at Belfort and he is twenty-four. He is antimilitarist and he has always sworn that if war should be declared while he is doing his service he will shoot his lieutenant. His lieutenant happens to be my other brother.

Amazar was inclined to discuss the futurists. Marinetti and his group, he explained, stand for a political protest, the protest of Milan, the machine city of dynamic force, against the museum cities, in which there is little industrial activity. In his campaign Marinetti has glorified the dynamic. His satellites practically limit themselves to the expression of the dynamic, which is symbolized by the automobile or the airplane. Pratella expresses this idea in his music, Baccioni in his sculpture, and it is because of this, rather than for any artistic reason, that Marinetti associates his name with theirs. He does not understand music or painting — he has told me so himself — but he understands dynamics. He loves noise and he loves war because it is noisy.

Ducie Haweis, long a resident of Italy, gave her sanction to this opinion, adding that the futurists also were violent against women and were determined eventually to bear their own children.

Of course, Italian women are usually dreadfully dull, I remarked.

They exist only for one purpose, she declared.

Then we tried to make a list of famous Italian women, aside from opera singers. A few, like Petrarch's Laura or Dante's Beatrice occurred to us, but even these existed only as the names of women great men have loved. There was, of course, Duse, but she had lived a life of almost complete negation. In the realm of literature one solitary name occurred to us, that of the not too illustrious Matilda Serao. Italian women do not appear to have left a deep impression on history.

The new movement, Amazar went on, aside from its political significance, which is Marinetti's contribution, is not of any importance. It derives from nothing and nothing will come of it. The painters seized upon the accidental in Cézanne as a clue to follow. I say accidental, because the deformation in Cézanne's drawing was something he could not avoid. Sometimes it fits into his composition. More often it stands out incongruously. Matisse has told me a thousand times that if he could he would draw as perfect a line as Ingres. He simply can't. His lines are all deformed and so an accident becomes a battle cry. Picasso, of course, is the cleverest of the new crew. His ingenuity is devilish and he will probably outlast all the others.

Amazar went on to talk about Renoir whom he said he considered the most complete of artists, complete in his life as well as his art. Cézanne and Francis Thompson, on the other hand, were artists who were weak in their lives. Cézanne bound himself to the Catholic Church to protect himself, to hold himself in, while Francis Thompson wrote The Hound of Heaven out of his weakness.

Nevertheless it is a great poem, Edith corrected Amazar. Thompson was the kind of man who put all his strength into his art.

This is a pretty accurate account of the tone of the

atmosphere and conversation in the Villa Allegra near Florence on the last day of July and the first day of August 1914. I do not think any of us, except perhaps Edith, had any definite realization of the tremendous events about to take place. Edith certainly had an uneasy instinct. She spoke a great deal about Wells's book, The World Set Free, which predicted the contemporary catastrophe, but set it fifty years ahead, and she said and repeated: Just think, the world will never be the same again. There will no longer be property. In the new society that is to come the socialists will have their way. She also predicted, not unreasonably, a Chinese invasion of Europe and America.

III

Sunday, August 2

Late in the morning, I called on Edith who was enjoying her colazione and reading the paper on the balcony outside her bedroom. She informed me that Germany had declared war against Russia.

Isn't this just like Florentine journalism? she demanded, exhibiting the second page of the sheet she held in her hand, a page devoted to a description of the cathedral at Arezzo, the façade of which had only recently been completed.

A little later she asked: Where is Marinetti? He wanted war and here it is. Where is *he?*

Edith drove to Amazar's for dinner and Ducie Haweis

and I accompanied her as far as the Via del Proconsolo, where she sent another cablegram to Reed requesting him to come along and bring gold, as she feared it would soon be difficult to cash cheques, and silver and paper money would be valueless.

Monday, August 3

I awoke with a dreadful sense of doom and an over-whelming desire to get back to New York. Everything seemed to be wrong with the world. From the Florentine paper we learned that the Germans had automatically declared war on France by entering Luxembourg. The Belgians and the Dutch were mobilizing.

In a desultory way Edith was preparing to leave the Villa. Doubtless her mood should have been allied to that of Madame Ranevsky in The Cherry Orchard, but it wasn't. She even spoke casually of the possibility that the invading Austrians might sack the Villa. She put a few objects away and left orders that all the books should be stored in one room. This was to protect them from the American signora who was expected to arrive in October with six young girl pupils. Of course, the signora and her pupils never came.

There was no formal farewell to the Villa or to the gardens. As Edith left, she said, I'm glad I don't want *this* any more. I've done it all, sixteenth, and seventeenth, and eighteenth century art. I've made a perfect place of this and now I'm ready for whatever will come after the war. I am through with all property, as every one else will have to be.

This was a little dramatic, but I daresay she meant it.[1]

As we were leaving, a cablegram arrived from Reed in Portland, Oregon: Coming will cable boat later.[2]

Edith, Ducie Haweis, and I started off for the station with two owls in cages, which belonged to Boyce Hapgood and Edith's son, John Evans, a bag for Edith, a hat-box for Ducie, a bag for me, my two canes and an army cape, and a package or two. Ducie was dressed in dull army blue, Edith in white, I in my green Norfolk suit. We were on our way to Vallombrosa to join Neith and the children at the Albergo Paradisino, where it is reputed that Milton wrote a part of Paradise Lost.

At Cook's we had bad news. Money was getting tighter and there was a rumour abroad that all Italian boats had

---

[1] At any rate from that hour to this she has never set foot in the Villa. One bright October day in 1928, fourteen years after the events recounted above, Fania Marinoff and I drove out to the Villa from Florence. No one had occupied it since 1914 and it was largely dismantled, as both Edith and Leonard had sent for quantities of furniture and pictures, and yet when the caretaker opened the windows and the sun poured into the gracious rooms, it was easy to reconstruct the past.

[2] This was the beginning of the journey which ended several years later with his death in Russia and his burial in the Kremlin.

stopped sailing, which would mean that no more mail from outside would reach us. Somewhere along the Via Tornabuoni we met Amazar and Lili with more bundles. They looked very sober. Amazar, in face of the news, was uncertain about going to Vallombrosa. He was inclined to believe that it would be more sensible not to spend the money as it might be a long time before he could receive more from America. Edith, however, persuaded him to come with us.

At the station we learned that the train — it was the through train to Rome — was half an hour late. We registered a trunk for Mabel and my unwieldy bag. The owls, we were informed — it was extremely difficult for the station-master to make us understand this — must have tickets of their own.

The train was crowded, but we managed to secure five places in one compartment by requesting a lady to move into another compartment, which she consented to do none too graciously. There remained with us two men and another lady, Italians. The lady's blotched skin was powdered a chalky white. She was dressed in white and wore many heavy pieces of jewelry including several pairs of rings. One of each of these had belonged to her husband, Edith deduced, and when she became a widow she had inherited his set. This lady began a flirtation with the Italian facing her and before long they were exchanging addresses and conversing in an animated fashion.

SACRED AND PROFANE MEMORIES

It was a hot day. The owls stared down at us from the baggage rack and contributed their share to the sense of doom which seemed to hang over us oppressively. Only Amazar and Lili laughed. The rest of us could not imagine why. Ducie read the Trend. Edith and I smoked cigarettes in chains and were silent and irritable. The train stopped, but not for long. Nobody paid any attention. Suddenly, as we were pulling out, Ducie screamed, That's our station we've just passed! That's Sant' Ellero. It was too late. I suggested jerking the bell-rope which would stop the train, but one of the Italians in the compartment warned me laconically that this act would mean at least a year in prison. Meantime the speed of the train was increasing. Ducie was extremely apologetic and stopped reading her magazine. After all, we had counted on her and she had failed us. It was my first visit to Vallombrosa; Edith previously had always driven there in an automobile; Leo had always walked.

Edith laughed. I wonder, she mused, a trifle bitterly, if we are on the road to Rome? I am always going to Rome by accident.

Amazar rang the bell to summon the conductor. That official, when he arrived, informed us we would not be obliged to go all the way to Rome. We could get off the train, if we so desired, at a small town near by where there was no hotel, but it was possible we might find a conveyance there in which we could drive back to Sant'

Ellero. Our alternative course was to go on to Arezzo to pass the night and to take the train to Sant' Ellero in the morning. Favouring this latter plan, we paid the extra fares.

Directly we had left the train at Arezzo, where we arrived about six o'clock, it became evident that a fiesta of some kind was in progress. Poles from which garlands and festoons of flowers depended lined the streets and the four sides of the piazza. Squares of red and gold and blue and silver brocade hung from the windows and balconies of the houses. The populace of Arezzo was celebrating the completion of the façade of the cathedral in a festival which would endure a week. It was the announcement of this event, strangely enough, which had caught Edith's eye in the Florentine Sunday paper. Subconsciously, perhaps, she had then and there determined to visit Arezzo. Naturally we found the town crowded. Eventually the manager of the Hotel Stella succeeded in finding one room for Edith and Ducie. Amazar, Lili, and I later secured two more rooms at the Hotel d'Ingleterra on the piazza. While we dined in the garden of the Stella, we made an unsuccessful attempt to persuade the owls to eat meat. Posters on the wall announced a performance of Perosi's La Risurregione di Lazaro in the Church of San Francesco. I proposed hearing this oratorio, but was informed that the second performance had been postponed until the following day.

I asked Amazar if he had ever been in Arezzo before.

He replied in the affirmative. It was one of the towns he found sympathetic. There were several things to see, the most important, perhaps, the Pieros in San Francesco.

From Edith poured forth a constant reiteration of the refrain: Do you realize this is the last night? This made me feel like Boule de Suif or the school children in Daudet's La Dernière Classe. Outside, however, it was gay. The Italians seemed to have forgotten all about the war. We walked up the hill — Arezzo, like so many other Italian towns, is exceedingly picturesque — to the cathedral which stands on a platform of stone, approached from every side by steps. In the park opposite there was an exhibition of moving-pictures and a great assembly had gathered to see them.

After the others had gone to bed I continued to roam about the town. Up the side-streets there were more moving-picture shows. At the Teatro Petrarco, opposite my hotel, the local company was performing The Waltz Dream. There were people everywhere. In one of the cafés near by a group of men sang a patriotic air in lusty unison. It seemed more in the manner of Germany, somehow, this song and this singing, but in Germany, of course, the men would have sung in harmony.

Tuesday, August 4

We woke early. The train for Sant' Ellero left at seven and breakfast was difficult to procure at six. Coffee turned up at last, but without butter or rolls. Amazar and Lili, having decided they would return to Florence later in the day, stayed in bed. The rest of us gathered our bundles together. Before I joined Edith for our departure, however, I made a stealthy expedition into San Francesco, where mass was being celebrated in one of the side chapels, to see the Pieros. The church had been reconstructed for the performance of the oratorio. The altar had been removed and scaffolding erected over the choir to seat the chorus, but I ducked under this and stood, in the few brief minutes at my disposal, feeling very mean, sad, and uncomfortable in the cold morning air, examining the faded frescoes, several, I recall, representing war scenes, by that Umbrian primitive, Piero della Francesca.

The news in the morning papers was the opposite of reassuring. The situation obviously was becoming more and more serious. I who had been in Italy but a few days already wanted to escape. On the train to Sant' Ellero I painted such a dismal picture of our prospective future to Edith that she actually urged me to go on back to Florence, while she and Neith descended from the train at Sant' Ellero. She had now determined to send Neith and her two children and her own son John to Holland as quickly as possible to embark on any boat of the Holland-American Line that might be sailing.

SACRED AND PROFANE MEMORIES

IV

In Florence I began by fortifying myself with a cocktail at Giacosa's. Then, leaving my army cape and my walking stick there, I went forth to gather a good deal of disturbing information. At Cook's I was informed that they were no longer booking tickets on trains further than the border, that literally hundreds of Americans were waiting at Domodossola to be permitted to enter France, some of them even sleeping in the streets, and that no boats were sailing from *any* port. At the offices of French, Lemon, and Company, I learned that only one American Express Company draft from each person could be cashed. It was impossible to cable for money because all the banks were closed. Even when the banks reopened it was proposed to limit withdrawals. French money had dropped to about one-fifth of its proper value.[1] Only the day before in Mc-Quay's Bank, Edith had experienced some difficulty in cashing a cheque. One of the officers of the bank, the tears streaming down his cheeks, had said to her, It's war, that's what it is, war! Already soldiers are being slaughtered by the thousands. And now, Charles Eyre, of French, Lemon, and Company, one of Edith's personal friends, was obliged to refuse when I asked him to cash her cheque for two hundred dollars.

You say she is at Vallombrosa. Tell her to stay there,

[1] It has remained there ever since.

he advised me. They know her and she couldn't be in a better place. His last words were reassuring: Even if the war goes on, this money scare will blow over in time.

All this, and even more, I tried to explain to Edith at one o'clock, but I had forgotten to take the siesta hour into account. I was reminded that the girls in the central telephone bureau would not return to work until three. So I went to call on Miss Galvin, a nurse Edith had brought with her to Italy to act as a kind of secretary. I had Edith's instructions to inform Miss Galvin that she would provide her return passage, and I did so. Miss Galvin replied testily that she would require a great deal more than that. She told me she had only twenty-five dollars left, her pension rent was due, and she needed funds to move. Everybody, she said, was leaving the pension to save money. Groups of four or five Americans were arranging to live together in single rooms in which they would sleep and do their own cooking.

My errands accomplished, however unsatisfactorily, I decided to start off once more for Vallombrosa. At the station, the station-master remembered me and smilingly inquired after the owls. On this occasion I did not pass Sant' Ellero, but descended from the train, took the rack and pinion railway, with its superb views, up to Saltino, then drove in a carriage through the pine forests to Vallombrosa. Centuries ago the monks planted these pines in straight rows and now the bare trunks rise to incredible heights before the branches spread, forming a canopy of green needles overhead, so that the effect is that of a natural cathedral. I have always wondered if Adolphe Appia saw this forest before he designed his sets for Parsifal in which the forest merges into the temple in the transformation scene. At last I arrived at the Albergo Paradisino, the inn that was once a monastery. My friends were eating dinner when I arrived, but Edith came out to greet me. All during dinner I went on telling them the news, news received with obvious dissatisfaction by Boyce Hapgood, due largely, no doubt, to the fact that he was amusing himself none too well here, and received more eagerly by the excessively nervous John Evans. Neith Hapgood lay awake another night.

Wednesday, August 5

In the morning Edith and I drove to Saltino. She dispatched another cablegram to America and we telephoned Florence only to corroborate the fact that no boats or trains were leaving Italy. She also sent a letter to Margherita Petti at the Villa Allegra with orders to close the Villa and dismiss the servants on October 1 if the American signora did not arrive, and it now seemed improbable that she would.

From the papers we gathered that there had been an engagement in the Mediterranean between German and English ships. The Strait of Gibraltar was being patrolled by the English. The Russians were believed to be fighting the Germans in the North Sea, the Germans were marching through Luxembourg, and the English were landing troops in France. No one who was not there, or in some similar locality, at the time can imagine how fantastic all this news seemed to us on the top of a sunny, peaceful mountain. We saw nothing, of course, but the Italian papers in which the news had been severely censored. No information could come through, naturally, without the consent of France, Germany, or England. Russian news simply did not exist.

Edith made the most of all this. She announced not only that she expected war between the allies, Austria and Italy, which still preserved what was called euphoniously in the newspapers "nostra sacra neutralità," but also a Chinese invasion, and she constantly reiterated her conviction that America would be dragged into this " last world war."

Amazar had said two nights earlier that he thought this war would do away with the post-impressionists and Edith agreed that the world and its ideas would be so completely altered that art as we knew it could no longer flourish. How do we know, she questioned us rhetorically, what people will want after this war? If they still continue to read stories and go to plays at least they will have to be different from the kind we read and see now.

As it became more and more doubtful if the banks

would pay her any more money, Edith emphasized the necessity of practising economy. She began then to speak of the possibility of our renting some peasant's or villager's cottage where we might all live together. She had in mind, it developed, theoretically, to be sure, a sort of communal scheme which if carried out to its ultimate conclusion would result in our alternating as cooks. On this day then Edith and I walked to the Saltino post-office to meet Ducie Haweis. Edith wanted to talk these matters over with her.

Twice a day, invariably, Ducie, who now with her children inhabited a Swedish cottage on the further side of Saltino, visited the post-office to inquire for mail. She made an unforgettable figure with her grey-blue eyes, her patrician features, her waved black hair, parted in the centre. Tall and slender, her too large ankles were concealed by the tight hobble-skirts she wore. Her dresses, of soft dove-coloured shades, or brilliant lemon with magenta flowers, or pale green and blue, were extremely lovely. Strange, long earrings dangled from her artificially rosy ears: one amber pair imprisoned flies with extended wings. It is very easy to recall Ducie as she tramped along the dusty roads of Vallombrosa, enveloped in a brown cloak trimmed with variegated fur, scarcely able, thanks to her tight skirts, to move one smartly shod foot in front of the other.

On this particular day she was emerging from the door of the post-office just as we marched up. So the three of us seated ourselves on a bench in front of the building, which, like post-offices everywhere, attracted all sorts of people who did not expect mail but who loved gossip. All three of us were smoking Macedonia cigarettes.

This would be a strange thing to be doing in front of the Provincetown post-office,[1] was my comment.

I'm inclined to think, Edith replied, as she looked around at the staring yokels, that it is considered strange here.

When we asked her for information about empty peasant houses, Ducie replied that she knew of a villa in the mountains. Edith did not receive this suggestion with enthusiasm. It was her idea that we find a house in the contadino village Donnini further down the mountain slope towards Florence.

I've often thought of doing something like that, Ducie remarked, but you would be obliged to build a house for the peasant before he would let you have his. These villages are constructed on strictly economic principles. There are no empty houses. There are no empty rooms. When a room is actually needed, it is added. Besides, Edith, these houses are infested with very lively vermin. I don't think even white-washing would help much to get rid of these.

---

[1] Perhaps I should explain that my remark was made in reference to the fact that in those far-away days ladies, who were just grudgingly being granted permission to smoke in hotel dining-rooms, were not in the habit of smoking publicly in the open air.

SACRED AND PROFANE MEMORIES

These days were very comic opera. Later in the afternoon we gathered, Ducie, Edith, John Evans, and I, at an outdoor tea-place situated in an ugly hollow between Saltino and Vallombrosa. Tables, laid under the trees, were guarded by two unsubstantial looking tin lions, the size of police dogs, stationed at either side of the shed where the refreshments were kept. Here we sat, late in the afternoon, frugally drinking water. After much whining, John Evans succeeded in persuading his mother to buy him fifty centissimi worth of ice-cream.

A little later I accompanied Ducie to her Swedish cottage, a small and unsightly red and buff house. Brought from Sweden in numbered sections and set up here, entirely out of harmony with the landscape or the neighbouring cottages, it commanded a view of the magnificent plain below: even Florence was visible, gleaming in what appeared to be a shower of golden dust in the late afternoon light. Ducie interviewed her cook in an attempt to discover if we could rent rooms at Saltino. She also discussed the possibility of laying in stores of flour, beans, and oil, the cook to prepare one plate of beans or pasta for each meal, so that we might all take our meals at her cottage. This latter proposal the cook scornfully rejected, but she informed us that it would be a simple matter for us to rent rooms at Saltino at fifty lire a month per person.

When I passed this information on to Edith later, she exclaimed, Oh well, let the whole thing drop. We'll stay on at the Paradisino. A contadino cottage, yes: that is something, but three rooms opposite the Saltino post-office in a building where they get up to make bread at two o'clock in the morning, never!

That was the end of our little economies. From that hour on we had wine with our meals, cigarettes, and even carriages in moderation.

V

Thursday, August 6

Most of the guests at the inn were Italian countesses, marchionesses, duchesses, each with a child or two. These Italian noble ladies all looked and dressed alike. They had pretty, fatuous faces, expansive bosoms and buttocks. They wore black skirts, white silk or linen blouses, quantities of huge diamonds on their fingers and in their ears, and black hats waving with white ostrich plumes. Among the children, little girls were in the majority. One boy, Sandro, had three sisters. He occupied the whole of their nurse's attention, refusing to obey her and yelling lustily when she pulled him about and cuffed him. There was a constant battle between the two and when these battles reached their climaxes, the sisters also screamed. Their pretty Italian mother ignored these broils.

Other guests at the inn were an Italian lieutenant who donned his uniform for dinner, a lady who was fond of strumming Madama Butterfly on the piano, and a few

Americans, one of whom, at least, was ejected because she could no longer pay her bills.

VI

My feeling most of the time was one of anxiety, insecurity. I did not unpack. I did no writing. I was waiting for some catastrophe which never actually occurred. On this particular day, Neith and I learned by telephoning from Vallombrosa that two Italian steamships were booked to sail from Naples on August 10 and 13, but that all the available passages were booked. I managed to persuade Edith that we should all go back to Florence on the morrow to secure passports and to find out what we could do towards returning to America.

Friday, August 7

A very early start brought us into Florence at eight o'clock and, although we had already taken coffee at the Paradisino and Sant' Ellero, we felt the need of another cup at Giacosa's. I added a cocktail to the coffee.

Italy was mobilizing, in spite of her vows of " sacra neutralità." Soldiers in uniform, with knapsacks, ready to go to the front, swarmed in the streets and, more formidable still, we saw a cannon on its carriage being dragged along by horses.

At nine o'clock we visited the office of the American consul to register our names for sailings.

Write down the name of your nearest male relative, was the sardonic suggestion of the Italian assistant to the consul, and if you are killed we shall know whom to notify.

The office was crowded with Americans who were looking for solace and succour. According to a notice on the bulletin board, our Secretary of State, William Jennings Bryan, had cabled to discover the whereabouts of one Florence Montgomery, but the United States Government did not appear to be officially alarmed about any one else.

Edith explained our case. We had in our possession return tickets on the Holland-American line, tickets now valueless because these boats were no longer sailing. A solution to our problem did not seem to occur to the consul. He nodded his head wearily while Edith talked and then advised a man standing behind her to remain in the interior, not to go to Venice.

On the bulletin board, along with the query about Miss Montgomery, a notice announced that the American consul at Naples had chartered a ship, but even as we were examining this notice, it was removed from the board. The consul's wife, with the air of the wife of a college president at an important reception, bustled about telling this one and that one what papers to sign and where to sign them. Dressed in black satin, with six willow plumes waving on her hat, she doled out cheer and advice to the frightened Americans huddled together in her husband's office. Patting the young girls on their shoulders, she addressed them as dearie, advising them to save their money if they had any. The boy who registered my name and address on the waiting list for boats was unable to spell Vallombrosa. These Italian names are as strange to me as they are to you, he explained. There was, as yet, no sign of panic. The general mood was rather that of listless despair.

A visit to Cook's elicited no further information. Neith and I drove to the Villa Allegra to collect some articles we had left behind and found Margherita in a furious temper because she had been dismissed. While Neith packed a trunk, Margherita showered unflattering epithets on Edith's absent head. The end of a regime is often more disturbing to servants than it is to masters.

We were all pretty tired when we returned to Vallombrosa and Edith went to bed immediately. Neith and I ate some food inattentively before we retired. Edith had found a letter awaiting her from Miss Galvin which ended characteristically with: Cheer up, dear. The U. S. A. is doing all it can for us all and we'll soon meet again in God's own country.

VII

Saturday, August 8

Waiters at the inn told us they had been ordered out. Perhaps they would not actually be called upon to fight for some time, but in case they were, the inn would close automatically. If Italy did not declare war at once, the inn would remain open later than usual, at least until October 1, to take care of the noble Italian ladies who did not wish to return immediately to Rome and Milan.

Sunday, August 9

According to the papers the Belgians were still holding their own against the Germans while the French were marching into Alsace. The French Government had awarded the badge of the Legion of Honour to Liège and had changed the name of the Rue de Berlin at Paris to the Rue de Liège. Japan, it appeared, would fight beside her ally, England, and there seemed to be trouble in Egypt. I suggested that it might be a good thing for me to return to Florence the next day to investigate, but Edith was opposed to my doing so.

Monday, August 10

A cablegram arrived from Fania Marinoff, informing me that she had landed and inquiring if I were safe. Neith received a letter from the consul in Florence advising her to be waiting in some port in readiness if she wanted to sail. Naturally I was more than ever impatient to get back to Florence where at least one could pick up an occasional bit of news. Neith wanted to go to Florence too. It was on the way to Naples. Edith objected. There won't be any boats for weeks, she argued, and it's much too hot in

Florence for the children. This idea of yours is simply ridiculous, Carl. Neith countered mildly, But they may take the trains off, Edith. The consul will never notify us unless we are on the spot. It is no good to wait out here so far away from the centre of things. We are sure to miss something. . . . And so on, pro and con. . . . At last Edith said rather feelingly that she did not respect my judgment, whereupon Neith became silent. I left them together and later in the day Edith informed me that I was to go back to Florence.

Tuesday, August 11

Off for Florence at twelve-fifteen. When I arrived I learned a good deal in short order. The French were fighting the Germans at Mulhaus, but news from Belgium had suddenly been cut off. More scheduled trains were being discontinued every day on account of the mobilization and subsequent transportation of troops. The Banco di Napoli had stopped payment. Two boats had sailed from America to pick up Americans in Italy. The warship Tennessee was sailing for Falmouth instead of Genoa as originally announced. It was rumoured that Assistant Secretary Breckinridge, with $2,500,000 in gold to be distributed at various ports, was on board. The American Express Company continued to cash small cheques. If Italy declares war, the consul informed his people, all Americans will be obliged to leave the country at once. He did not announce how they would be able to accomplish this evacuation. An order was issued at the post-office making it imperative that cablegrams be signed with the full name of the sender. A rumour was abroad that all but one of the ocean cables had been cut. There were said to be 10,000 Americans stranded in Italy, 2,500 in Genoa alone. Pension and hotel proprietors were taking advantage of this situation to force up the rates.

For six lire I engaged a room at the Pensione Rigatti, 2 Lungarno della Borsa, largely frequented by Americans. The padrona was a nice old lady with several new bookcases full of new books about Emanuel Swedenborg and the Bible. Her guests included Hogarth Pettijohn, a young Yale man in Florence on a scholarship to copy Botticelli and Titian, a couple of school-teachers, and a soldier tenor, who frequently entertained his fellow officers with a song after dinner while somebody played his accompaniments on a very bad piano. The tenor's name was Dino Borgioli.

It was very hot. I spent a few moments on the roof garden, a feature of the Rigatti, and then went to bed to sleep badly. Jangling church-bells in a campanile just across the court outside my room made a terrific din. The mosquitoes were active and lusty. The humid heat was all but unbearable. I snatched a little rest before dawn.

SACRED AND PROFANE MEMORIES

Wednesday, August 12

Americans learned on this day that Italian banks would no longer recognize cabled drafts from the United States Treasury. Most of them would have been less astonished if the sun had split in two and dropped into the sea. One such mad one rushed into the midday coolness of Giacosa's, where no one spoke or even understood English, to cry: What do you think? The Italian banks refuse to recognize the United States Treasury! Such a thing has never happened before in the history of our country!

About noon I ran into Arthur Acton, as suave, as debonair, as fatalistic, as witty, as sardonic, as calm as ever. He summed up the situation: If the war were ended today, it would take sixty years to straighten out the world's affairs and even then they would never be where they were before. Then, encountering Mavrocordato and Mrs. Acton's brother, Mitchell, we walked across the street to the Banco McQuay where Mrs. Acton, very smart in a black and gold costume with a hat jaunty with plumes, was endeavouring to send some money to her children, Harold and William, who were in England in charge of a nurse. Acton had tried to go to them by automobile, but he had been turned back at the border. Mitchell had been motoring in Germany when war was declared. His car had been confiscated and he had been obliged to walk a distance of fifteen miles, luckily no more, with two ladies who found themselves in a similar predicament. We stood in Lowe's small office in the Banco McQuay: Mrs. Acton, brisk and businesslike, Arthur, ironically smiling, Mitchell, querulous, and Mavrocordato hovering over the group like some great bird of prey. Lowe was talking to Mitchell: My dear man, I will let you have my car on credit, you may move my piano out of my drawing-room — you are welcome to it — but I cannot loan you five dollars.

Acton followed this up by announcing that he would be delighted to invite me to lunch, but in these times they believed in making what was left over do for dinner. Mavrocordato then said that two-and-a-half lire was the limit which he spent on one meal, as he could draw no more money until August 20, when five per cent of his deposit, the amount he is permitted to withdraw, will be four hundred lire.

Acton told me that the Roslings, fortified by passports and passwords, were going to attempt to reach England. After they crossed the border — if they succeeded in crossing the border — they would be obliged to travel on what train — cattle or soldier — they might be able to climb aboard. Acton said they were leaving because they were getting tired of watching Rosling's mother die. She was doomed six months earlier, but had lingered on. They were entrusting her to Acton's care and, as the funeral follows death very closely in Italy, he was obliged to inquire whether they preferred burial or cremation.

Thursday, August 13

Edith did not come to Florence as she had promised she would. John had a fever, and she was not feeling well herself.

In the afternoon I attended the meeting called by the consul. Twelve or fifteen men, of the type who like to meet and march, were present. The occasion was as solemn as the panelling of a jury. The consul announced that he had called us together before the general meeting the next day because then there might be women present who were likely to interrupt. He was quite frank about his purpose in addressing us. In a few days, he said, mail will be coming through again and the consulate will have enough to do in attending to its regular business. In the circumstances I suggest that you gentlemen take over this problem of stranded Americans. He then cheerfully proposed the election of a chairman, a corresponding secretary, a treasurer, and the appointment of committees.

In the street outside I ran into the Braggiottis. I received a letter from Edith asking me to take care of the children, Lily Braggiotti said to me, but I don't see how we can do it. If there is war we may be obliged to go to America. Besides we have eight children of our own. If the others were *nice,* English children perhaps it might be managed. Yes, we shall stay on here if we can. If the pupils go we can do our own work. We live very simply on polenta, beans, and peas. . . . In her peculiarly languid manner she moved away towards the little yellow pony chaise, followed by Isadore Braggiotti in white flannels, pink shirt, and turquoise studs and links.

Friday, August 14

Neith telephoned from Vallombrosa that Edith was still sick. She had heard from Reed who was sailing Saturday.

The meeting in the afternoon was held in the rooms of the Società Filologica, above the bureau of the consulate. The room was crowded and it was very hot. I recognized a few familiar faces. The Braggiottis were there. Mrs. Acton's brother sat in a conspicuous position and was elected vice-president. Every kind of election was held except for that of a class poet. The whole business of the meeting was carried on in so low a tone that no one back of the first two rows could have heard anything, and yet there must have been nearly two hundred persons present. The effect was that of a low mass. Pettijohn took advantage of the mumbling to invite a pretty stenographer to go out with him for an ice later, but she refused, explaining that she would be obliged to work.

Before dinner in the salone of the pension, Pettijohn was playing Der Wacht am Rhein which happens to be the Yale Alma Mater song.

If America goes to war with Germany, I'm afraid Yale will have to change that, I suggested.

143

Yale has so broadened the scope of that song that it has lost its original significance,[1] was his reply.

Strolling along the Arno I watched a tanned Italian fisher-boy, bare-legged and nude to the waist, go out in his boat. At the fortezza two men twanged guitars beside the basin while other boys danced together on the gravel, their long shadows assuming queer shapes under the strong arc-light.

I passed another sleepless night. It was very hot, the mosquitoes again were energetic, the bells tolled endlessly, longer than usual towards dawn in honour of some fiesta or other. I felt as if I could not tolerate Florence another

---

[1] Bright College Years, written by Harry Durand in 1881 and sung to the tune of Der Wacht am Rhein, has by common consent been Yale's Alma Mater song since that date, and closes concerts of the Yale Glee Club and meetings of the Yale alumni. Many other songs have been written for the purpose of displacing it: Alma Mater, words by J. K. Lombard, music by Thomas G. Shepard, in 1893; Brave Mother Yale, words by Charles E. Merrill, music again by Thomas G. Shepard, 1903; and Mother of Men, words by Brian Hooker, music by Seth Bingham, written in 1908 to win the prize offered by John Oxenbridge Heald. None of these songs was successful.

During the war and for several years after, however, Bright College Years was discontinued. Again prizes were offered for a substitute. Several hundred manuscripts were submitted, but none was accepted. Some ingenious person suggested that Bright College Years should be sung to the tune of the Marseillaise. Efforts to replace the old favorite gradually waned. It is still the official Alma Mater song.

day. It was all too tiresome, the same faces, the same round of places: Cook's, French, Lemon, and Company, Giacosa's, the Consulate, and the Gambrinus. Had it not been for Benozzo Gozzoli I think I should have ended by hating Florence.

*   *   *   *   *   *

VIII

Friday, August 21

Summer rain is unusual in Italy, but the night we came into Naples was as wet a night as I can remember anywhere. It had rained all the afternoon in Rome and the rain had followed us south, drizzling dismally against the window panes of the railway carriage.

As we emerged from our compartment, very tired and irritable, we seemed to be advancing against a glad, gay army. The station was crowded with Neapolitan soldiers ready to entrain to Rome. They were gay, I say, and singing, after the habitual manner of Neapolitans, as they pushed themselves into the carriages waiting to receive them, in spite of the fact that danger lay immediately ahead, for it seemed certain that some one expected to leave Naples had been marked for death. On the three preceding nights bombs had been laid on the track. Three trains had been partially wrecked and many persons badly injured.

Edith Dale, her twelve-year old son, John Evans, Neith

Hapgood, her two children, and I had fled from Florence to the coast. It was not, however, our intention to sail immediately. There was a possibility we might visit Amalfi; Capri was discussed and Edith, in prospect, related many quaint stories of Cinquecento Charley and Elihu Vedder, the kings of the island of the azure grotto. In the meantime we planned to stop a day or two at Naples.

We walked out of the station — an incredible distance, reminding me of walks in the Grand Central Station in New York during its reconstruction days — to emerge in a glare of yellow light illuminating the wet pavement, now crowded with shrieking cocchieri, shrill barkers for hotels, and frenzied porters, always demanding more soldi than they received, all of whom doubtless, after the manner of Naples, seemed noisier and more active than they actually were.

Without hesitating, Edith dived into a cab with two horses. Neith Hapgood followed her more languidly and then the children, John Evans with a shot-gun, Boyce Hapgood with an owl — the other owl had died — and Beatrix, hopped in while the porters installed as much of the baggage as could be accommodated. They filled the cab, which presently drove away, leaving me behind with two suitcases and the vague information tossed back at me by a departing Edith that she was bound for a hotel the name of which apparently began with a B. The driver I engaged said it would be Bertolini's. Drives in the night in strange cities always seem longer than they really are. This drive seemed interminable. The cab was closed and through the windows I was afforded only fleeting glimpses, as we passed a lamp, of the darkened streets of Naples. The rain poured down and it was very damp and chilling. It was not long before we began the ascent of a hill. I had heard wild tales of the perils of Naples and it occurred to me to wonder if I were being abducted for ransom. In the end I resigned myself to what was apparently a limitless climb. It must be Vesuvius, I muttered to myself. Edith has decided that we shall pass the night in the crater to get dry! Eventually, we stopped before a lighted tunnel which, strangely enough, proved to be the entrance to the hotel. The other carriage had arrived just ahead of us. A doorman guided us through the tunnel to a lift which carried us up to still higher altitudes. The exit opened on a proper hotel corridor. We entered another lift, descended two floors, and were shown to our rooms.

Saturday, August 22

With the rise of the morning sun I got my first magnificent view of Naples and the bay from my balcony. Down beyond the long vista of tawny houses and green trees, the ultramarine Mediterranean gleamed in the sunglare. A boat with two funnels was slowly steaming out of the harbour. To the left Vesuvius smoked.

I ordered breakfast, but it was exactly one hour before coffee, honey, and rolls arrived. Later, I learned the reason for this delay. With the departure of the tourists — and with what expedition they had vanished at the first rumours of war — and the calls for soldiers, the hotel force had rapidly melted away until actually at the present moment one waiter was serving, as well as he could, the few guests who remained. Directly after breakfast, the manager visited us to discover how many of us would require lunch, explaining that each morning the cook went marketing with his basket to provide precisely the amount of food necessary for each meal.

Dropping accidentally into a casual conversation with two gentlemen in the corridor of the hotel, I discovered they were both sailing that very night on the San Guglielmo. They assured me, moreover, most solemnly that this might be the last chance to leave Italy — although the Canopic might get under way on September 12 and one or two smaller boats were announced for later departure. On the day when Italy declared war, however, they reminded me, any or all of these ships might be requisitioned for government service.

The San Guglielmo, it appeared, belonged to the Pierce Brothers who operated her on a line known as the Sicula Americana. In times of peace she was employed to carry Sicilian and Neapolitan emigrants from Naples to Brooklyn. This steamship, with two others of the same line, had first been brought to my attention by a notice posted on the bulletin board in the office of the American consul at Florence. It was stated that they had been refitted to accommodate stranded Americans who would be taken back to their native land at the purely nominal rates of $110 to $150 a head. What price the Sicilians and Neapolitans were accustomed to pay to voyage on these vessels I do not know. For purposes of comparison, however, I might state that the contemporary price for a steerage passage on the Mauretania, palatial accommodations, relatively speaking, was $35. The Pierce Brothers apparently were privy to the fact that this was war time and that the alternative methods of escape from Italy were impractical.

Later Edith, Neith, and I drove through the sunny streets of Naples to the consul's office to find it crowded with chattering Americans who had escaped from Austria and Switzerland, temporarily reduced to penury by the fortunes of war. There were also a few of those more fortunate ones who were assisting the stranded. I know that one man gave away $2,000 during the course of the morning. The consul probably was helpless. In addition to his natural incapacity for dealing with so desperate a situation, he had recently burned his arm severely and he was carrying it slung in a bandage. He could give us no further information than that we already possessed. His advice to every one was to get out of Naples as quickly as possible. We left him a trifle impatiently to pay a visit to the office of the Pierce Brothers.

Here, after a sufficiently prolonged wait, we were granted an interview with a benign, young Englishman who described the San Guglielmo with that steady reserve in statement and manner that always leads me on to death and destruction. Certainly, he affirmed, she was an emigrant ship, but she had been entirely reconstructed to meet the present crisis. Partitions had been erected between the bunks. The floor had been painted. A dining-saloon had been arranged: the typical voyagers on the San Guglielmo, it appeared, had been accustomed to visiting the kitchen, plate in hand, for their daily pasta. New bedding had been supplied. There were a few officers' quarters which had been sold at a higher rate, but any passenger would be permitted the run of the boat. I would suggest, he concluded, with great earnestness, as he leaned towards us across the counter, that you inspect the ship and judge for yourself. She is now in the harbour. Neith was in favour of acting on this suggestion. I was instinctively opposed to it. If we inspected the boat in advance I am sure we would never sail on her, was my argument.

Neith agreed that this was sound reasoning and so, without further consideration, we paid down 2,200 lire for passage for Neith and me, Boyce, Beatrix, and John Evans. This arrangement concluded, Neith and Edith left for the Bertolini to eat lunch and pack. I stayed behind to collect the registered trunks we had not yet called for in the baggage-room of the station. In the remaining moments at my disposal I visited the Naples Museum.

About four o'clock in the afternoon I arrived at the dock with two trunks. The sight that met my eyes was amazingly lively. There were men changing lire into dollars, occasionally doling out counterfeit American money, screaming frantically as they waved their greenbacks to advertise their calling. There were fruit-vendors, hawking their wares on land and in boats, audibly advertising their lemons, oranges, peaches, pears, grapes, and plums. There were dealers in steamer-chairs, hastily improvised from rough boards and canvas and offered at three to four dollars each. There were merchants of pots, pans, wash-basins, and cups. I myself saw one of these refuse two lire for a common tin receptacle. There were beggars: blind beggars, lame beggars, armless beggars, deaf beggars, whole and powerful beggars, all vociferously demanding soldi. There were numerous Americans, and more were arriving every minute, making an effort to arrange to have their baggage carried aboard. There were frenzied, shrieking porters begging to be allowed to carry this baggage. Indeed, everybody on the dock appeared to be gesticulating and screaming either in Neapolitan dialect, or in Italian, or in good or bad English.

A porter offered to carry our trunks on board, a distance of fifty feet, for two dollars. I neglected to engage him.

Subsequently I employed another fellow who swore he had rescued me from the first robber. Presently this one staggered on board with the two trunks and disappeared. A mass of humanity swallowed him up and I could see him no longer. It occurred to me that perhaps the trunks were lost. Had they been my own, I would have forgotten about them, but they belonged to Neith Boyce and so I went on board to search for them. I could not find my porter on deck. I could not find my cabin when I went below. The very idea of cabins was new and a little absurd to the stewards and crew of the ship. Besides, as I learned later, many of the crew were embarking for the first time. There was no order, no system. A state of chaos prevailed. Three times I asked an officer of the company to inform me of the location of my cabin. His preoccupation was so complete that apparently he was ignorant of my very existence although I bellowed the question quite into his ear. My porter was lost together with the trunks. Apparently I had no cabin. In the circumstances I determined to disembark, a brave project which proved difficult to execute. The mass of persons on board wholly prevented free movement, and the white-coated attendants who might have created aisles of egress were obviously quite unable to assist me. One of these fellows standing by the entrance to the passenger gang-plank informed me that he had received orders to permit no one to descend by this path. He added that I must go down by the way the baggage was coming up. I gave a rapid glance over my shoulder along the thirty feet of deck that separated me from this other way out. It was swarming with passengers and sailors, strewn with trunks and suitcases. I inspected the indicated gang-plank: a steady stream of men in single file marched up its narrow confines. To descend by this route meant fighting against the obstruction of heavy trunks on powerful shoulders. I quickly made up my mind that insanity was the only practical method with which to meet this emergency and straightway projected myself into a fit. Rolling my eyes, I staggered and screamed lustily. I fought with a sailor who attempted to control me. I kicked out right and left. Presently I found myself back on the quay where I pushed over boys who stood on their heads and struck an armless child who begged me to put a penny in his mouth. I cursed volubly in English and bad Italian, taking the names of numerous gods and saints in vain. The force of the sudden rush away from me precipitated several persons in the water. It was at this dramatic moment that my porter caught sight of me. Signore! he cried and, looking up, I located him sitting on the two trunks on the upper deck. Fighting my way back up the gang-plank, I reached his side and rewarded him with two lire.

No, he protested, this is a ridiculous amount. I rescued the signore from the robber who would have charged him ten lire. I certainly deserve more than two.

In face of my obstinate refusal to give him any more, he went away scowling and muttering, presently to return with a factotum for one of the hotels. The porter says he prevented you from being robbed, this one explained. You have not paid him enough. He is a bad character. He is bad even for Naples where everybody is a little bad. You must give him more money or he will do something to you.

What will he do? I demanded with a spontaneous display of interest.

I will put the trunks back on the quay, the porter cried.

This threat was effectual. How much does he want? I inquired weakly.

He wants three lire.

Giving him the amount he desired, I fell back against one of the trunks, exhausted. At this moment I caught sight of Neith in her dark blue cape, leading Beatrix by the hand, walking slowly towards me down the dock. The others followed. . . .

September–October 1914.

THE HOLY JUMPERS

THE HOLY JUMPERS

I

Time hangs heavy on an ocean voyage. Thinking becomes almost a necessity. One may read, of course, the books he never finds the leisure to peruse elsewhere: Jean-Christophe, or Don Quixote, or Clarissa Harlowe. Surely the three-volume novel of the mid-Victorian era was invented with the ocean traveller in mind. Twenty chapters more to make the book last from Liverpool to New York, many a poor novelist must have groaned, and it is pleasant to realize that certain contemporary novelists, such as Theodore Dreiser and Romain Rolland, are creating books of a suitable length for an ocean voyage.

In the end, however, reading at sea becomes tiresome. The unsettled monotony of the waves begs the voyager to lay down his book now and again so that he may reflect. So he ponders over the proverbial and considers the obvious. No great problems are ever solved at sea. I am certain that Tristan und Isolde was composed on land. Gunpowder and sewing-machines must have been invented there.

On my way to the Bahama Islands recently,[1] it was not

[1] This voyage was undertaken in the company of my wife, Fania Marinoff, who was visiting the Bahamas as the star of a

long before I tired of such literature as was available —
Francis Grierson, H. G. Wells, and St. John Ervine were
the authors represented — and sitting in my deck-chair
alone, watching the flying fishes play, I allowed my mind
to wander. There was the slightest swell on the tropical
oily water, but no breeze blew over it. Dante once wrote
lines to the effect that in unhappy moments our minds
revert to happier occasions. In this excessive peace it pleased
me to recall more exciting hours.

My earliest Christmas tree held its place for a moment
in recollection. Followed, a memory of my first pair of
trousers and a succession of fires, for the first of which I
was responsible. It had no important results. On the occasion of the second, a few months later — I must have been
about eleven years old — my mother awakened me, in the
hours following midnight, to announce that the barn,
in close proximity to the house, was burning. One look
out of the window was sufficient to completely arouse me.
I had possessions which were dear to me, live chameleons
and sundry copies of works by J. T. Trowbridge and
Horatio Alger, Jr., but I did not think of them at this

---

motion-picture organization which planned to utilize the
island of Providence as "location" and the Negro population
as extras for a film called Nedra. As an amusing footnote to
these facts I might add that I appeared briefly in this film as
the officer of a warship, the director having neglected to engage
a proper actor for the rôle.

time. Unhampered by burdens, I made my escape from the house, not yet on fire, clad in my nightrobe and two un-mated stockings of my mother's. In spite of my efforts with the garden hose to prevent the fire spreading, the flames, weary of the barn, eventually consumed the house. Some years later when, as Paris correspondent of the New York Times, I occupied a room in the Daily Mail building on the Rue du Sentier, an oil stove exploded in the office adjoining mine. The walls and ceiling of my room were constructed of clouded glass and presently, when this glass began to crack, I grasped a pad of type-writer paper and a derby hat belonging to a visitor and made a very speedy exit into the street. Once I have felt the cold steel of a revolver pressed firmly against my forehead. I who am ignorant of the art of swimming have capsized in a sailboat in a heavy sea. I have twice been run over by automobiles. . . . However, I reflected, it is perhaps from art, and not always the best art, that I have received the most memorable thrills. I can never hear the Dies Irae in Verdi's Requiem without jumping and there is a chromatic phrase in César Franck's tone-poem, Les Eolides, a caressing sensual passage which I cannot even remember without shivering. The opening bars of Richard Strauss's Don Juan have for me the nerve-edging trick which is in the power of cocaine. There was a trombone player at Coney Island . . .

It further occurred to me that it was very fortunate

that thrills could be arranged. Otherwise it is probable that many individuals would go through life without experiencing any. Most Americans are stimulated by a baseball game; others require the added fillip of a pugilistic encounter or a wrestling match. Bull-fights act as a catharsis for the Spaniard, while a Frenchman may have his pulse lifted, if he so desires, by an execution by guillotine. Everywhere the individual and the mass are searching for excitation: revolution, fast motoring, war, feminism, Jew baiting, airplaning, Alfred Casella, the Russian Ballet, and lynching are a few of the more conspicuous public opportunities to heat the blood.

II

After a three-day voyage we arrived at Nassau, the çapital of the Bahama Islands. Early one morning, as the dawn broke softly through the pink-flushed cloud banks, we entered the beautiful harbour. As prismatic as a black opal, streaks of emerald, amethyst, and the most vivid indigo succeeded each other in the transparent water. In the depths, over the clean white sand, one could see the quivering sea-garden alive with brightly coloured fish; here a sea-wasp, a filmy, inverted globe ready to sting the swimmer, and there the white belly of a hungry shark. The coast showed a low line of hills on which squatted pink and yellow plaster houses with green blinds. Every-

where the fronds of palm trees waved. We landed near
the public park, crowded with Negroes, more fully clothed,
was my first impression, than seemed essential or even
proper in the tropics, and shaded from the sun by spreading straw hats. There were a few white men in the group.
Now the low plaster houses shone very pink, yellow, and
green in the hot sunlight. In this clear atmosphere, the
white shell roads sparkled like silver snakes while the
black natives seemed carved from ebony.

With a splendid carelessness Providence has sprinkled
New Providence — so the early settlers identified the
island — with vegetation. Everywhere, in rich man's garden and by the poor Negro's hut alike, the most magnificent trees flourish, growing rankly out of the thin layer of
soil which clings to the coral underneath. Nowhere is there
order, nowhere is advantage taken of opportunity — in
fact it is well-nigh impossible to engage labour in force,
so prodigal is the country in natural gifts, so lacking in
disagreeable climatic disturbances that it is unnecessary
for any one to make extra exertion. On all sides, one next
to the other, rise cocoa palms, date palms, royal palms —
of which there is a stately avenue in the garden of the Hotel Colonial — palmettoes, guava, the jelly-bearing, trees,
sea-grapes, cocoa-plums, bread-fruit trees, producing great
green loaves, which when boiled taste like sweet-potatoes
and not at all like bread, silk-cotton trees, the roots of
which ascend five feet or more above the soil and assume

curious shapes like those of dragons or fantastic crocodiles, orange trees, grape-fruit trees, royal poncianas, with their scarlet blossoms, long seed pods, and leaves of delicate fronds in myriad shades of green, alligator pears, bananas, rubber trees, sapadilloes, plantains, sugar apples, Spanish limes, almond trees, and banyan trees.

Nassau boasts few industries. The principal one is sponge-diving and many boats are consecrated to the divers. There are also few amusements, aside from those furnished by nature. The bathing is magnificent. There are several excellent beaches on the island of New Providence. By crossing the harbour one comes to Hog Island, a narrow strip of land separating the harbour from the open sea precisely as Venice is screened from the Adriatic by the Lido. The bathing on the ocean side is what I have described as magnificent. The ocean here is no mighty monster. The transparent water is always warm and always calm, even in roughish weather, because of a bay formation. The slope of the beach into the deep sea is gradual. Occasionally a sea-wasp stings the swimmer. In the deeper water there is said to be danger from sharks and side-cutters, although naturalist authorities assert that the shark is shy of approaching so large a shape as that of a man if it is in motion. Fishing is scarcely a sport here. One may even catch sharks in the harbour. Tropical fish with strange names, such as Passing Jacks and Goggle Eyes, come to the very quay edge to nibble at the hooks baited with conch that small boys dangle from short poles, and one may observe them in their glittering splendour below in the water, almost as clearly as later when they lie, still moist and quivering, in baskets at the market.

Through the medium of a boat with a glass bottom one may visit the very sea-gardens of the ocean depths, planted with brain corals, sponges of sensational size, waving sea-fans of amethyst and amber, rose sea-anemones, the chrysoprase branches of sea-plants, and coral caverns, in and out of which strings a solemn procession of staring, wide-eyed fish, some with speckled sides and ruby gills, others with garnet and sapphire fins, sad, thoughtful, resplendent fish, in this radiant garden, gleaming in the colours of jewels: turquoise, aquamarine, jade, chalcedony, beryl, opal. I have seen the gardens surrounding the Villa Gamberaia near Florence and the palace gardens at Hampton Court, the gaily formal gardens at Fontainebleau, and the melancholy Luxembourg Gardens, where George Moore met Mildred, but none of these has ever appealed to my imagination as did the sea-garden of the Bahamas. It might have been just here that Sadko encountered the Princess of the Sea, for it was surely of some similar spot that Rimsky-Korsakoff dreamed when he wrote the ballet of the petits poissons aux écailles d'or et d'argent.

Aside from the pleasures afforded by the sea, the stranger will derive entertainment from walking through the streets of Nassau, past the sidewalk vendors of fruits, with their baskets of yellow and gold and green balls, past the cock-sellers, lightly balancing flat baskets of fowl on their heads, past the charming houses, hung with Bougainvillæa, the owners of which are protected from the sun by dropped jalousies, past the churches, of which there are many, set deep in fragrance and shadow. Negroes everywhere, all walking with the peculiar slouch and talking with the peculiar drawl indigenous to the British West Indies. There are quarters devoted to them, Grant's Town, Fox Hill, and Free Town, and there you may see street after street of picturesque huts, some of them with thatched roofs, but the Negroes live anywhere they please — and can afford to — in Nassau, and clerk in all the shops. There are a few mulattoes, dubbed Conchy Joes, because their colour is akin to that of the conch shell, but blacker blood predominates.

The Governor of the islands, a Scotchman, has not very long been an incumbent of the office.[1] Each night as he dines in his bungalow, set on the most perfect site on the island on the highest rise of ground, with a charming pink wall enclosing it, a bagpiper reminds him of his beloved homeland by playing Scotch airs on his instrument, as he marches round and round the veranda. The first time I heard these pipes my imagination directed my fancy towards the Orient: the hot, peaceful night, the palm trees, the blinded bungalow, and the wailing melodies, all

[1] These lines were written in 1915.

suggested the Far East, but it was not long, especially when I closed my eyes, before I was reminded of Scotland, and it was doubtless for this reminder that the Governor had imported the piper, who had blown the pipes, I was informed, in the Great War until he was wounded, when he had been sent to Nassau on a furlough.

All views of the bungalow were pleasing, had it not been for one detail, a repulsive statue of Columbus, directly in front of the main doorway, a weak attempt at the swashbuckling and the picturesque. I know of only one other statue in Nassau, that of the young Victoria in front of the Houses of Parliament, as the modest assembly buildings are vaingloriously called. I have seen worse statues of the late queen in London. I have never seen anything worse than the Columbus statue anywhere.

III

In the evening of the first day, besought by a Negro to take a drive in one of the phaetons which are the conventional conveyances of the island, we passed through Grant's Town, the huts of which, set among banana, palm, and silk-cotton trees, were dimly lighted. Then we followed long stretches of dwarf, plaster walls, like the walls in Tuscany, until at last we came to a structure built in the form of a tabernacle, the thatched roof of cocoa-palm leaves upheld by posts. The sides were open. The ground was strewn with dried palm branches. On a platform at one end of the building, a preacher exhorted his brethren. Behind him sat a group of elders and deaconesses, the pillars of his church, while below extended row after row of black faces framed in gigantic straw hats. Still other worshippers stood outside. Our driver informed us that this was a meeting of the evangelical sect known as the Holy Jumpers. Descending from our ancient vehicle we found seats in the tabernacle.

Your time has come! the preacher was shouting. You've got to come to Jesus if you want to come at all. He suffered for you and you've got to suffer for Him! Climb in the chariot! Hustle up the golden stairs! Kick those devils down! Shove 'em off! Don't let none of 'em come near you! Don't you hear Him calling you all? Oh, God, give these people into the keeping of Jesus!

Hallelujah, amen! Glory to God! Yess'r! Preach it! were shrieked from the benches.

The preacher's effects were varied with the nicety of a Mozart overture. There were descents into adagio and pianissimo, rapid crescendos and fortissimos. Slowly, slowly, the assemblage was worked upon and as the speaker progressed in his exhortation he was more and more frequently interrupted by shrill, distorted cries.

Is there a sinner among you? Let him stand forth! If there is one without sin down there I don't know who he is! Come, brothers, before it is too late. Repent! Repent! The time of Jesus' glory is at hand.

O God, take a poor sinner! wailed a treble voice.

Hallelujah! Amen!

O Jesus! Lamb!

Glory to God!

Some one on the platform started the hymn, Oh, what a wonderful life! and soon the voices all joined in, growing more and more resonant, richer and richer in spirit and feeling. Now a contralto dominated, now a high tenor, now a bass, but what harmony, what volume of tone, what an attack! After a time another hymn followed and then another and finally, without a break in the singing, the tremendous and awful Hiding in the blood of Jesus, a variation perhaps of Washed in the blood of the Lamb. Now the congregation swayed to the pronounced rhythm it was creating. From side to side the lines of huge straw hats swayed. Back — and forth. . . . Back — and forth. . . . Hiding in the blood of Jesus. . . . Back — and forth. The rhythm dominated us, ruled us, tyrannized over us. The very pillars of the tabernacle became unsteady. A young black woman rose and whirled up the aisle, tossing her arms about jerkily. O God, take me! she cried as she fell in a heap at the foot of the platform. There she lay shrieking, her face hideous, her body contorted and writhing in convulsive shudders. Heads here and there wagged swiftly out of rhythm. Moans and hoarse cries mingled with the terrible, inexorable singing. The heads swayed, a few wagging swiftly out of rhythm. Back — and forth. . . . Hiding in the blood of Jesus. A young girl fell flat on her back in the centre aisle. She was near enough to me so that I could see the circle of foam forming around her lips. Her teeth were clenched, her fists set tight, her arms and legs executed unreasonable gestures. Now a deaconess from the platform was bending over her. The Lord is coming to you! she shouted. Take him in! Hear me, take Him in! Get rid of your devils! Shake 'em out! Open your mouth and receive the Lord! . . . The initiate continued to shriek and struggle. Inarticulate, meaningless sounds emerged from between her clenched teeth. The foam reformed around her lips. The nerves in her epileptic ankles seemed to be raw. . . . The congregation swayed. Hiding in the blood of Jesus! Back — and forth. . . . Back — and forth. The deaconess grew confidential. You got to come, she almost whispered. You got to come. You don't want to be a wicked sinner any longer, do you? Come! Come! Come! Come! Come! Come to the Lord! Open your mouth and take Him in. . . . Ai! Ai! shrieked the poor sinner. . . . Hiding in the blood of Jesus! Back — and forth. Back — and forth. Back — and forth. . . . Here He is. He's coming! He's coming! . . . The stooping woman herself became hysterical. Her eyes rolled with excitement. Supreme pleasure was in her voice. The crisis was approaching. It seemed as if the girl lying prone was in a frenzy of delight. Every muscle twitched, her nerves seemed to be raw, her finger-nails dug into her palm. Uncontrollable and mystic cries, unformed obscenities struggled from her lips . . . and then at last a dull moaning and she lay still.

IV

How closely the ecstasy of Negro sanctity approaches sorcery. If he had seen the Holy Jumpers, would Huysmans have altered his famous description of the Black Mass? According to Remy de Gourmant, the author of A Rebours would have welcomed such first-hand experience. Le messe noire est purement imaginaire, writes the French critic in the third series of Promenades Littéraires. C'est moi qui cherchai les détails sur cette cérémonie fantastique. Je n'en trouvai pas, car il n'y en a pas. Finalement, Huysmans arrangea en messe noire la célèbre scène de conjuration contre La Vallière pour laquelle Montespan avait prêté son corps aux obscènes simagrées d'un sorcier infâme.

Next day at breakfast, black Priscilla at the hotel expressed her opinion.

I'm a Baptist, she said. I don't hold by those jumpers. The females jump and the males jump after 'em.

September 23, 1915.

LA TIGRESSE

LA TIGRESSE

1

New York, which Henry James once referred to as " the long, shrill city," of all the cities of the world I have lived in, delights me most.[1] Some cities I always dislike; some, like Florence or Cincinnati, I find agreeable for a week or a month at a time, but there is a shifting grace about Manhattan like the changeless, changing pattern woven by the waves of the sea, which is persistently and perennially attractive. Moreover, there are overtones which awaken memories. When one is in Paris one is in Paris; when one is in Amsterdam one is in Amsterdam; when one is in Munich one is assuredly nowhere but in Munich, but it is possible to be in New York and a great many other places simultaneously. Shut away from your sight the buildings that surround the Public Library and you are in Imperial Rome. Further up Fifth Avenue certain millionaires have reminded us that there are châteaux on the Loire.[2] The Giralda Tower of Seville [2] looms in leafy Madison Square, "Diana's wooded park," as O. Henry lovingly described it, and near by a fair copy of the Venetian campanile pierces the sky. A little removed on Fourth Avenue there

[1] This is still my feeling.   [2] No longer, alas!

is a very good imitation of the Torre del Mangia in Siena. Where Canal Street strikes off from the Bowery in the heart of Jewry the sweeping colonnades which preface the Manhattan Bridge unmistakably suggest the colonnades of St. Peter's at Rome. The Arch of Titus guards Washington Square. The chalets which serve as stations for the elevated railroads remind us that the Swiss Family Robinson lived in a tree. The Town Hall of Verona decorates Herald Square.[1] There are buildings on Lafayette Street and on East Forty-third Street obviously inspired by Venice. On East Broadway, between brick tenements and lofty buildings, smart brick houses with white doorways topped by fan windows, marble steps, and handwrought iron railings with polished brass finials, carry us back to London or New York of the fifties. At certain seasons of the year violets[2] or roast chestnuts are vended on the street corners after the manner of Paris. A veritable Egyptian pyramid caps a building on Nassau Street. Here and there one catches a glimpse of a Dutch façade. The " diners " awaken thoughts of London coffee stalls, including Neil Lyons's immortal Arthur's. The lovely eighteenth-

[1] More than half of this charming structure has been demolished to make way for a taller office building.

[2] Since the performance in 1926 of a play by Edouard Bourdet called The Captive, in which a Lesbian presents her friend with violets, florists, as well as street-vendors, have found it practically impossible to sell these lovely flowers in New York, so sex-conscious, apparently, is the female population.

century City Hall, perhaps the most beautiful single building in New York, is surrounded by skyscrapers, like a Taj
Mahal in a valley dominated by mountain peaks. Now the
war has set a camouflaged battle-ship with fighting turrets
in the centre of Union Square, otherwise a wilderness of
moving-picture houses, saloons, and burlesque theatres,
and at several points, at street intersections or in parks,
Iowa farmhouses have been erected in which the Salvation
Army or the Knights of Columbus dispense hot coffee,
doughnuts, and the Saturday Evening Post to soldiers and
sailors. If these incongruities cause no comment, it is because the note of incongruity is the true note of the island.
Nothing is incongruous because everything is. In a city
where one finds a Goya Apartment House and a Hotel
Seville it is no surprise to discover that an avenue has
been christened after Santa Claus! New York, indeed, is
the only city over which airships may float without ap-
pearing to fly in the face of tradition. I might safely say,
I think, that if a blue hippopotamus took to laying
eggs on the corner of Forty-seventh Street and Broadway
every day at noon, after a week the rite would pass un-
observed.

So in New York it is possible to eat in seventy or eighty
different styles: in Spanish restaurants on Pearl Street,[1] on
the sidewalk, after the fashion of certain European cities,
on Second Avenue,[1] in Rumanian style on Forsythe Street,

[1] No longer, alas.

the food of the Syrians on Washington Street, Turkish or Armenian fashion on Lexington Avenue, Swedish fashion on Thirty-sixth Street, Russian fashion on Thirty-seventh, German on Fourteenth, Japanese on Nineteenth, Hawaiian on Forty-seventh, Jewish on Canal, Indian on Forty-second, Greek on Sixth Avenue, and French, Chinese, Negro, and American almost anywhere!

So cosmopolitan is New York in the matter of cookery that no bizarre appetite should go unsatisfied: gefüllte fish or venison, sharks' fins or bear steak, snails or pirogue, grouse or tel kadayif are all to be found somewhere.

In these strange restaurants, all so foreign to the spirit of America, and yet all somehow so *right* in Manhattan, bearing nostalgic breaths of the homelands to those who frequent them, strange adventures occur, a thousand un-chronicled episodes happen in a night. It is well to remem-ber in this regard that New York is the city where John Masefield worked as a barman, where Harry Thaw shot Stanford White on a roof garden of White's own designing, where P. T. Barnum first exhibited white elephants and aged Negro women, and where later he became the im-presario of Tom Thumb and Jenny Lind, where Adah Isaacs Menken, the lady who wrote Infelicia, dedicated to Charles Dickens, and who, in her impersonation of Ma-zeppa, was bound to the back of a horse which dashed madly over the canvas crags of a New York stage, lived at what later became the Maison Favre,[1] where Nick Carter worked, where Van Bibber sailed in swan boats, where Steve Brodie jumped off the Brooklyn Bridge, where Chuck Connors ruled Chinatown, where Gorky was refused hotel accommodations and Marie Lloyd was held at Ellis Island because they had neglected to marry their consorts, where Theodore Roosevelt, returning from a journey around the world, drove up Broadway in a triumphal procession like an emperor in his chariot, where Emma Goldman,[2] William Dean Howells,[2] Theodore Dreiser, Victor Maurel,[2] and David Belasco[2] make their homes and do their work.

II

It was a sweet sight, the tall, ungainly young blond French savage in his naval uniform, very naïve, standing to sing in the crowded café. We had earlier invited him to sit at our table to consume a little of the popular red wine of California, so that when some one suggested that he sing Madelon he got up to do so at once as if there were no other course open to him after having accepted our hospitality. His high-pitched and unresonant organ pro-

[1] This picturesque French pension, located at 528 Seventh Avenue behind the Metropolitan Opera House, is now no more. The actual table d'hôte, presided over by Madame Favre herself, was a great haunt of celebrities in pre-war days. I occupied the first floor front during the years 1907–10.

[2] No longer, alas!

duced sounds wholly unrelated to the art, or even the pastime, of singing as it is generally understood, but he knew the words and he continued to deliver stanza after stanza in his quaint schoolboy manner, lifting now his right arm, now his left.

Quand Madelon vient nous servir à boire . . .

The buzz of conversation in the café ceased and began again, ceased and began again. Jean-Baptiste (why are all French peasants named Jean-Baptiste?) continued,

Quand Madelon vient nous servir à boire . . .

Was this the twenty-first time? When he came to the stanza about the caporal,

Un caporal enkepi de fantasie . . .

we felt we had listened long enough for the sake of politeness and went on with our conversation, but Jean-Baptiste continued to sing:

Ma-de-lon, Ma-de-lon, Ma-de-lon . . .

It is a better war song than America or England has produced, Peter Whiffle was saying. Both words and music are far better than those of Over There or Tipperary.

It is very long, was my comment.

Elle rit, c'est tout l'mal qu'elle sait faire . . .

sang Jean-Baptiste and suddenly, quite as suddenly as he had commenced, he finished, and sat down to drink more of the good red wine of California in the most complete silence. He had sung all the stanzas he knew and unless some one asked him to repeat them, which doubtless he would willingly have done, he could do no more for us. Eventually, however, Peter Whiffle, observing that the boy seemed out of our circle, brought him back in again with a question: Qu'est-ce que vous faites au pays?

Jean-Baptiste became garrulous: Sometimes we have rabbit stew. When my sister was married we had rabbit stew. For weeks beforehand in preparation we caught cats on the roads, in the fields, in the barns. My brother caught cats and I caught cats and my father caught cats: we all caught cats. We caught forty cats, perhaps fifty cats. Some were huge tomcats, some were females with kittens inside them. Some were black and some were white and some were yellow and some were tabbies. One cat scratched a big gash in my brother's face which bled. My father and I shut the cats in a room — my brother was afraid to help us after he had been scratched — and we went in after them with cudgels and beat about us, beat the cats on the head. How they did howl and screech and fight, but we were a match for them. For an hour we chased them around the room, beating them, till all the cats lay dead on the floor. Then my brother and my mother skinned the cats and made a magnificent rabbit stew for my sister's wedding. . . . Jean-Baptiste lapsed into complete silence again, reverting to his glass of red wine.

It was growing late. A few sailors with their girls sat about at the tables chatting and drinking. The proprietor, a great figure of a man with shaggy eyebrows and the moustache of a villain of a tank melodrama, glowered from behind the counter. A young fellow occasionally tapped melodies out of the piano, American tunes of the day and night, and some of the sailors tried to dance, hobbling about clumsily, destroying rhythm and women's footwear.

The place brought a vague memory back which I sought to establish more vividly. Some past fragrance blew into my nostrils. . . . I tried to remember my nights in seaport towns. Spezia? Hardly. Nor Liverpool, nor Dieppe. Antwerp? There is a certain street in Antwerp where sailors are deprived simultaneously of their virility and of their money, a long winding street near the wharves. In the evening the windows, with tiny, square, bulging Belgian panes, are brilliantly lighted, but each of these windows is carefully curtained and only a chance shadow occasionally exposes a lewd movement in the interior to the passer-by. A fat figure decorates a doorstep now and again, and in the street one jostles a slovenly hussy or passes a sleek procurer with greasy moustache and eager eyes. Here and there a café interrupts the rhythm, a café where fat Belgian molls and drunken sailors, English, French, Swedish, and American sailors, make some pretence of gaiety. . . . No, the present scene was not like this. Perhaps it was the perfume of one of the women, and perhaps it was the way the sailors danced, but suddenly it all came back to me how once I had spent a quiet and delightful evening in a bourgeois café, a haunt of French sailors, near the Quai de Cronstadt in Toulon. There had been some singing, a great deal of talking, an immense amount of smoking and drinking, and it was all extremely cheerful.

The entrance of a pleasant looking little woman, obviously a personality, interrupted my revery. She wore a plaid skirt with a blue flannel blouse. Her frowzy hair was surmounted by an unfashionable turban. Her figure was inclined to stoutness. She was forty and she had a number of gold teeth, but her eyes were dark and piercing and her smile, as she turned to bow to one of my companions, was divine. I must have looked a question.

That is La Tigresse, he said.

La Tigresse?

I don't know her real name. Every one here calls her that. She lives upstairs and usually appears about this hour in the morning. She is very remarkable when she sings.

We invited her to sing at once, but some time elapsed before she did so. Passing from group to group, she asked sailors questions about their homes, about their lives at sea, about the women they met, about Paris. When she finally came to sit with us, I was struck at once by her essential dignity, her reserve, her poise. She spoke feelingly of the war and its effect on her beautiful France and she touched on more trivial topics, but whatever she talked about she was always interesting and charming, always to a certain extent a personage. She had, indeed, completely aroused my curiosity before she sang at all.

It was two o'clock. The crowd had thinned to three groups. The patron yawned behind the counter. The pianist had left. Suddenly La Tigresse arose and, backing into the centre of the floor, began to sing, without accompaniment, Quand je danse avec l'homme frisé, which related the history of a preposterous béguin in a frank and ribald manner. The tune itself had the self-conscious impertinence of the can-can from Orphée aux Enfers. Her hips swayed, her eyes flashed fire, her voice bawled out the tones. Singing, indeed, the woman became an artist. What fervour! What animation! What power of characterization! What sensuous appeal! With one song she had already evoked an atmosphere and she continued to hold us with her magic, singing now comic songs about a simple couple from Brussels visiting Paris, now tragedies of the water front, and then the dark and gloomy Seine flowed under the nocturnal bridges before our eyes and the vice and sordid misery of the rats who haunt the quays came between us and the reality of the café. Lower and lower she dragged us with unfailing effect, through the streets of Ménilmontant and Belleville. Bibi and Toto and Bubu and other bad boys stalked across her red and purple canvas. They loved and killed and died. In contrast to these sordid histories, she sketched lighter pictures of Paris smiling, tiny midinettes, saucy grisettes, and flamboyant cocottes, Madeleine of the Olympia Bar, Célestine of Maxim's, or Marguerite of Pagé's, or the love adventures of little Mimi Pinson on her way to work, overtaken by a shaft from Eros, shot from the window of a warehouse by a beau gars. All of these were painted with sympathy and understanding. The characteristic gesture was never wanting, nor were humour and pathos. I don't know how much she would have delighted me in the theatre, but here, a little under the influence of the good red California wine, in this small, semi-deserted room, with a few French sailors as a background, hers seemed the finest and most finished art. We ordered a bottle of champagne and when it bubbled in the glasses, La Tigresse sat down to help us drink it.

Who are you? I asked, in some awe.

La Tigresse. Have you never seen my name on the posters in Paris? She spoke freely of her triumphs in the small halls behind the Gare Montparnasse and her advance to the Scala and even La Cigale, where her successful representation of a femme cocher had caused the defection of the beautiful Idette Bremonval.

And now she was here, forgotten, singing in a cheap American haunt of French sailors and taken by them with less gusto than they would have awarded to the commonest Coney Island diva. Our applause, I thought, must have come to her as a great boon, giving her a delight she had not experienced for some time and yet from her appearance and manner as she sat at our table I could not make out that she was in any way excited.

The woman is a find, I said to Peter Whiffle later. She should have a great success if we could arrange some drawing-room appearances for her. As we discussed the possibilities of her making a more public audition a great pity surged over my heart, a pity for her warm but unfashionable apparel, the signs of her poverty.

We went back again and again to hear La Tigresse. She always came into the café around one o'clock to remain until the place was empty. Sometimes she simply tied a skirt around her nightgown, stuck a few pins in her hair, drew on stockings and low shoes, threw a black shawl over her broad shoulders, and descended from her bedroom; sometimes she wore the costume in which I had seen her originally; but each night she had a new repertory, each night she delighted us with new songs.

Peter and I agreed that something must be done. We were aware that French songs, no matter how good or how well sung, would make no effect in our music halls. I recalled, indeed, the lamentable failure of Yvette Guilbert to establish herself with the public of the Colonial Theatre on Broadway one sad Monday afternoon. A " recital " in Æolian Hall did not seem practical. We believed, however, that La Tigresse in her plaid skirt and blue flannel blouse might take on at once in somebody's drawing-room after dinner. This was to be her rehabilitation. In time, indeed, she might be able to return to Paris, to her old place in the halls there. So we dreamed and planned.

One night after La Tigresse had been particularly wonderful — she had led three apaches to the guillotine and four or five women to bed — we determined to speak to the patron about her, and we called this grave-faced peasant, this brawny fellow from the South of France, over to our table.

It's about La Tigresse . . . I began, rather awkwardly.

La Tigresse? . . . Well, there she is.

Yes, what can be done about her?

What do you mean: what can be done about her?

We want to get her some work.

Work! La Tigresse won't work. She doesn't want work.

We looked rather astonished, and I persisted, But surely if she were better known she could make some money. . . . Then she could buy herself some decent clothes. . . . She . . .

At last the patron understood and understanding, he began to laugh. Huge guffaws shook his enormous frame as he rocked back and forth. He shouted and puffed with merriment. Tears ran down his cheeks and mingled with the pomade of his moustache.

We stared at him in amazement and so did the few others who remained in the café. At last he felt calm enough to speak.

You think she's poor, he gasped, La Tigresse . . . ?

We nodded. Isn't she?

Good God! I'm prosperous. I do a good business. I've put away some money, but I'd like to have all the money that woman has! She was very successful in Paris and she saved her earnings. Later when twilight was beginning to descend on her talent — it is often very easy for even the proprietor of a café to be somewhat poetic when he is speaking French — she met an old South American. He gives her all the money she wants and asks very little in return. He sees her only three or four times a year because he is always travelling and La Tigresse detests to travel. She has a pearl necklace. She has a car. God, it's funny to think that some one believes La Tigresse to be poor!

Then why, I demanded, does she dress as she does? Why does she sing for us? Why does she come here at all?

It is her life. It is what she is accustomed to. It is what she likes. She was brought up in the bars of Toulon and her childhood was pleasant. So she comes here to revive the memory. The types are similar, as similar as one can find in New York. Her clothes are no disguise. She is comfortable in them. She always wears them. They are what she is used to. What would you have?

LA TIGRESSE

III

The night was cold. It was after three and the streets were deserted. The cold steel-blue of the sky was sprinkled with stars. It was very still.

Peter Whiffle spoke the first word.

What a wonderful thing to do, he was saying, as much to himself as to me, to revert to type in this way, or rather to refuse to relinquish type, to cling to it, to live with it, to caress and love it. She sees no reason for making herself uncomfortable merely because she is rich, and she is right. You've heard of men who, after they made their pile, bought the old farm back for sentimental reasons, but they never went to live on it. Nobody has ever done this before.

It's all very well for La Tigresse, I replied, as we continued to walk. If you know what you want you can find it somewhere in New York. But how are you and I going to revert to type, supposing we want to? What is our type? How are we going to settle back in our middle life into the pleasures of our youth? They have been too many. They have been too various.

Peter turned this over. I don't want to settle back and I don't believe you do either. If you do, you'll find a nice, little wooden house, very much like the one you were born in, I should fancy, down Union Square way. It's dedicated just now to the uses of the Salvation Army war activities, but the doughnuts would probably do more to make you remember the old home than the building itself.

It's too late to go there tonight, I announced, and to-morrow . . . Well, I'll think it over.

You bet you'll think it over! retorted Peter.

February 17, 1919.

FEATHERS

FEATHERS

I

Even in babyhood, it seems, I had begun to love cats. My mother records the fact in her diary, such a diary as mothers plan to keep when their sons are born, in which at first a daily entry is made, but which soon dwindles through short weekly reports down to a sentence or two a month, and eventually to nothing. On September 25, 1881, when I was a little more than a year old, my mother wrote of me: He seems very bright in imitating: he will bleat like a lamb, bark like a dog, or mew like a kitten. I think of all the things he has ever played with or seen nothing pleases him so well as a cat. Grandma has an old tortoise-shell and she seems to be willing to have baby fondle her as much as he likes even if he does rub her fur the wrong way sometimes.

My talent for imitations does not appear to have developed, but my warm feeling for cats has intensified with the years. I recall a blue short-haired cat which I carried around the house as a child, and then for fifteen years I was not permitted to possess another. My family compromised on birds, canaries and thrushes, alligators, chameleons, field mice, and turtles. Once, even, the door was opened to a dog, a fox-terrier named Peg Woffington, but never again to a cat. My passion for animals was so strong that I think something living was always beside me, but it was only much later in life, after I had left the home of my parents, that I became familiar with the animal I cared for most.

Since those early days a succession of cats has passed before me, cats who lived with others, cats in fiction and poetry. Some of these I have described, many I have not, for I hold a memory of many pleasant cats including Jessie Pickens's strange, brown tabby Persian, Dodo, with a snarl and a snap and a growl and a hiss for all the world, which terrified her, but always a kiss for Jessie. This puss crossed the Atlantic — in a cabin — seventeen times before she died. I cannot forget Anna Marble Pollock's dynasties of orange, white, and smoke cats. When I passed a week-end at her place on Long Island, Inky, a cuddling smoke, used to sleep with me. For many years two black cats lived together at a florist's in the Hippodrome building on Sixth Avenue. One, long since dead, was in existence when I first came to New York, the other, much younger, is still living, withal very old. When both were alive they were wont to lie together in the window, under the bowls of roses or the pots of ferns, assuming mediæval attitudes, recalling the sleek, black cats with dilated topaz eyes which once frequented witches' hearths, or they would sit in the doorway in the posture in which so many

FEATHERS

Egyptian cats have been immortalized. I have never gone by this shop without stopping to speak to these handsome ebony cats, abnormally large. Cats, indeed, are as personal as people, and ordinarily more memorable, as far as I am concerned. How often I have visited Mabel Reber to talk to her cats, the magnificent silver Jack Frost, twice the size of the average cat, with the eyes of a Raphael cherub, eyes of so frank and naïve a character that they seemed strangely perverse in a cat. His companion, Comet, I believe was even larger, a mammoth cat, a great red tabby Persian with butterfly markings and copper eyes, who lived to be nearly fourteen years old, with all his teeth, most of his energy, and the coat of a llama, a coat, indeed, which seemed to grow thicker as the years went by. Jack and Comet are angels now, hunting mice along the Milky Way, pursuing the shadows of phantom butterflies in the feline paradise. Then there was Avery Hopwood's Abélard, our companion on many an automobile drive, a friendly feline who purringly enjoyed the knee of any stranger. So, indoors, he lacked mystery, but in the garden, wandering among the pink cosmos and the purple dahlias, waving his flaring banner of a tail, he became a feral enigma of nature. There was Tom, an ugly, gaunt, grey tabby with a white belly, who took refuge in the cellar six storeys below our garret on East Nineteenth Street, merely tolerated for a year until a new janitor bought him a collar and fed him liver. The metamorphosis was astounding, both physically and psychologically. As Tom's belly expanded, his coat growing sleek and smooth, he began to pay an inordinate amount of attention to his toilet, polishing his nails assiduously and flecking the tiniest suspicion of dust from his whiskers. His walk became languid and dandified, his manner somewhat arrogant. In preference to walking, this cat employed the elevator and he would call out his floor in no uncertain voice. Emerging from the opened car, he would pay a visit to some favoured tenant, scratching on the door until he was admitted, when he would stroll around the apartment, examining new objects or searching for mice, until his curiosity was satisfied, when he requested permission to leave. Other cats of this period and locality come back to the memory: the cat next door, a handsome brown tabby, with a coat which shone as if brilliantine had been applied to it, lying in the sun on the stucco wall with the manner of a breathing sphinx, never venturing into the street, not even so far as the sidewalk, and permitting no alien hand to stroke his back. There were the black and white cats of Giovanni Guidone, the grocer, whose white faces were so curiously smudged with spots of black that they resembled clowns and indeed their behaviour intensified this impression. Above all, there was the blue short-haired cat with the white tip at the end of his tail who lived with a near-by delicatessen dealer. This grimalkin had learned to roll eggs from the counter so that they would break on the floor and he might eat the contents. He unfailingly chose, the dealer informed me, the freshest and most costly eggs.

As for my own cats, I still cherish an affection for the blue, short-haired cat of my childhood, my Paris cat, bereft of his tail, and delicate Ariel, an orange tabby Persian with a white belly, a soft, appealing cat who suffered from strange illnesses, an invalid from birth; but Feathers meant more to me than these others.

II

In the closing pages of The Tiger in the House, I have drawn a picture of Feathers about to become a mother. These paragraphs were written in good faith. Feathers, about eighteen months old at the time, had passed a weekend on Long Island with an orange tabby male and I had every reason to believe that the usual result would follow. It did not. Feathers died without issue. I am convinced, indeed, that she died a virgin.

I had discovered her one day, a tiny kitten, at a pet-shop. In a cage with ten or twelve companions, kinsmen or acquaintances, bouncing and rolling about like Andalusian dancers or miniature harlequins, she alone had chanced to please me. She gave me her absorbed attention when I entered the shop and she continued to gaze at me, a slight smile flickering about her eyes. As I gathered her into my arms, she playfully extended one padded paw, a paw out of all proportion to her diminutive size, and pressed it against my lips. This gesture won me so completely that, after the fashion of a Roman gentleman acquiring a desirable slave in the public market, I purchased her at once. This simile cannot be carried further for, after the manner of cats, she presently asserted her authority so impressively that in a few days such slaves as inhabited my garret were not garbed in fur. It is certain, Claude Farrère has written in his biography of the Chat-Comme-ça, that man is superior to the other animals, but it is also certain that the cat is superior to man.

She was a Persian pussy, but she never could have been exhibited at any cat-show where the rules were strict, for she was the logical outcome of misalliances and miscegenation. Not alone her mother, but also her grandmothers for generations back, must have been easy going. The evidence went to prove that these loose ladies had received visits from black gentlemen, from yellow gentlemen, and from white gentlemen, indiscriminately, for Feathers had a coat of many colours and, had she been a male, Joseph would have been her suitable name. In the circumstances, she might reasonably have been christened Iris. Her own name, which fell to her naturally enough in a few weeks — I never hurry to identify a cat — was derived from the long hairs which protruded from her ears, long, curly hairs, technically known to cat-fanciers as feathers. She was, as you may have gathered, a tortoise-shell: her fur was marked with splotches of the richest orange, the deepest black, the palest tan, but the splotches were not well-defined in the manner that judges at cat-shows demand of prize-winning tortoise-shells. Moreover, she had other markings. Some of the black hairs were tipped with gold. Her breast and nose were white and so were her paws, but her legs were barred (sinisterly, no doubt) with tabby stripes. She belonged, as a matter of fact, to that unclassified variety, the tortoise-shell and white smoke tabbies! So far as I could ascertain, she had no silver or blue blood, but she atoned for this lack, in a measure, by another peculiarity: she had seven toes on each paw and these twenty-eight toes were all fitted with claws. Her eyes, rather indefinite in colour in the beginning, later became a pale yellow. They were large, round, and intelligent.

Nevertheless, in spite of her mixed breeding and her scarcity of " points," she was a picture cat, beautiful in her teratological manner. Any painter would have been delighted to ask her to sit for him. As a kitten she was a tawny, orange, and black ball of fur, an exasperatingly roguish, ambulatory chrysanthemum with a ridiculous Christmas tree for a tail. She had, of course, even then, her moments of repose, of pensive reflection. I never can forget how, on her arrival in our garret, after the inevitable tour of exploration which any cat, however young and inexperienced, however old and brave, always makes in a new environment, I say I cannot forget how, with quaint dignity and grace, she settled herself at last demurely on a ledge underneath a table-top, curling her tail around her legs, and cocking her head at that angle which a robin often affects.

As she grew older, her grace and beauty developed and, very early in our acquaintanceship, she asserted her independence and displayed her character. Never seriously ill before her fatal sickness, she refused vehemently to take medicine when she suffered the minor ailments of kittenhood. Exerting all her strength to free herself, scratching the controlling hand, she would attempt to bite and, if still held, would growl and spit, as the hissing of cats is so cacophonously called. She possessed an extremely quick temper and any sort of restraint immediately infuriated her. Her growl was faint and rather ridiculous, but her spit, which required a considerable distortion of the jaw, was her last word, a word by no means to be taken lightly. On such occasions her face lost something of its ordinary beauty, a beauty which was never placid, which always included something of alertness in its make-up. Fortunately, she never sulked, never bore malice and, once restored to her liberty, forgave quickly. I do not think she would have forgiven a real insult or, from a stranger, even a fancied one, but she knew at heart that I was her devoted friend and presumably reasonably well-intentioned towards her. She indicated plainly, however, on more than one occasion that even well-meaning attentions would not be tolerated when they involved sequestration of any variety. All cats — almost all cats, at any rate — are independent, but Feathers made a fetish of independence.

In her own way, she was affectionate. She soon learned to come to the door to greet us, my wife or myself; indeed, the sound of the ascending elevator, were one of us absent, was sufficient to send her flying to the door. She disliked solitude, even if she were asleep, and so passed most of her time, when circumstances permitted, in the same room with either Fania or me, but she usually did not care to lie on my knee when I was sitting, and she would soon contrive to extricate herself from any kind of vulgar embrace. When one of us was lying down, however, she often found the belly an excellent place to nap on, never, curiously enough, after we had gone to bed. She had one tender trick which was original with her: if held in the palms of the hands she would lie, contentedly enough, on her back, with her great paws relaxed, or perhaps she would press one, padded and soft, the claws concealed and inactive, over an eye or over the lips, as she had done, indeed, on the day when I made her acquaintance. Occasionally she became paradoxically soft and yielding, lying on my knee in the most abandoned attitude, with one paw depending, limp, but she never liked to have her belly stroked and would use her claws vigorously to protect herself from this dishonour. Often she was feral. At times she seemed to fly from one end of the garret to the other, touching the floor as seldom as would Nijinsky or some flying-squirrel.

She never saw a mouse. Her hunting expeditions, therefore, were perforce directed against insects. She believed the airplane to be an insect. One of these giant craft flew frequently past my garret window and she never missed the whimpering buzz. Standing on her hind paws, she pressed her little rose nose eagerly against the pane and gave vent to the curious cry, so like the creaking of a rusty hinge, which always associated itself in my mind with her hunting. She never succeeded in bringing down an airplane, but she never missed a fly and she was expert at attacking moths. It was an æsthetic pleasure, a lesson in grace, to observe her catch one. Whenever I discovered a moth I cried, Feathers, come here! The tone was sufficient. From a sound sleep in the farthest corner of my garret she would come bounding, expectant, alert, a feverish intensity in her eyes, her ears pointed back, and the faint, quick mew of her hunting cry issuing from her throat. Then, as with my down-turned palm I would sweep the white, flying insect into her vision, she would leap for it, with one rapidly extended paw, sometimes following its flight to the top of the piano or a shelf of books. It was a joy to observe her perfect muscular control on such occasions. Once the moth was stunned, she permitted it to escape to give herself the pleasure of recapturing it; eventually, with every appearance of pleasure, she would eat it, and then she would purr.

She did not care much for toys; at any rate she soon tired of them. A celluloid ball, which rattled, amused her for a few hours. She leaped after it into the porcelain bathtub, following its clattering bounds with wild celerity, but after a few repetitions of this exercise she began to be bored. Presently, she was through and never condescended to notice the ball again. One object, however, invariably entertained her, a silly, simulated strawberry, of a type once worn on women's hats. She would carry this by the stem in her teeth from place to place, pouncing upon it, pushing it from her, gathering it towards her. If some one would play the game with her she would retrieve this strawberry. She also enjoyed another game which began by her establishing herself behind the crack made by an open door, lying in wait, and catching passing objects with her paw through the space beneath the hinge.

She liked to lie on my knee while I sipped my coffee in the morning. Almost invariably — she was never entirely consistent about any act — she came to me for a few moments after she had eaten her own breakfast. It is possible that this gracious ceremony partook of the nature of gratitude. Next, habitually, she took up her position on the cover of the soiled-clothes basket, adjacent to the bathtub, and appeared to be interested in our ablutions. This interest was not feigned, but it was directed towards her personal ends. She was waiting until we had bathed and the tub was empty, so that she might repose herself in its warm bottom. Sometimes when baths were unduly prolonged, in her impatience she encircled the ledge at the top of the tub, waving her tail in annoyance and making faint mews, occasionally almost losing her footing on the narrow, perilous, slippery path. As the last drop dribbled down the waste-pipe, she would leap in, lie on her back, and roll luxuriously on the heated porcelain. A few moments of this dissipation was enough to satisfy her. Leaping out, she began to wash herself in preparation for her morning nap. She honoured no one spot: sometimes she slept on Fania's lap, sometimes on top of the piano, sometimes on the floor.

She was not afraid of strangers, but she took no particular interest or pleasure in their presence. Her manner was perhaps more languid than usual, as though she were assuming a special social grace. Indeed, she entertained but one fear — she was an exceedingly courageous cat — and that was for storms. An ordinary rainstorm terrified her, a thunderstorm unbalanced her reason.[1] While the bolts were flashing and booming, she was wont to hide herself under the bathtub, under a bed, or behind some door, quivering with nerves, her ears laid back almost flat on her head, her fur awry. Such comfort as we could give

[1] A later cat, Scheherazade, would sit on the window-ledge and placidly observe the course of the wildest storm.

her was unavailing. Only with the ceasing of the storm did she regain self-control. This peculiarity she never conquered. Indeed, being a cat, she probably made no effort to conquer it.

Cats seldom break glass or china by accident, but it often amuses them to play with frail objects, pushing them off their foundations. Feathers never broke anything. Her grace was abundant and it was a pleasure akin to that of watching an expert trapezist to see her take a long and daring leap to a shelf on which reposed rows of glasses or cups without disturbing a single piece. One of these shelves, higher than my head, was ranged with unserried ranks of Venetian goblets. She was not destructive; neither was she secretive. Pens and keys might be left in plain view without arousing in her a desire to hide them. My Ariel, on the other hand, had caches under the corners of the rugs where she concealed every small object she could discover. Other habits of Feathers were less agreeable: she pulled the threads loose in a Daghestan rug and shredded the canvas backs of many scrap-books, sharpening her claws.

Like all well-bred cats, she was mostly mute. When she spoke, her voice was soft, almost, indeed, inaudible. Waiting in the morning outside our bedroom door for her breakfast, which she usually received at seven o'clock, she sat rigid and silent. When she was " calling," as the period of heat is poetically described by cat-breeders, her voice was as musical as the soft coo of a dove, which it somewhat resembled. She was very sparing, too, with her purrs, only lavishing them on exceptional occasions. She never overdid anything.

She had a fascinating habit of looking at me, without speaking, when she wanted something. She expected me to divine her wish and this was usually easy to do. It was as if she had reasoned: It is absurd of me to try to make him comprehend my speech, although I understand very well what he says. I'll simply wish very hard what I want and he will probably understand it sooner and more completely than if I had asked for it.

She was right. We had a very profound understanding and neither of us imposed on the other. Within the boundaries of our garret walls she was permitted to do anything she liked — even to play the piano at three o'clock in the morning, a pastime of which she never tired — and for the most part she generously allowed Fania and me the same privilege. In one respect, however, she was obstinate. She refused to tolerate the presence of a rival. This aversion manifested itself for the first time when I brought an orange kitten home. During the three days that the kitten remained in our garret she not only tortured him in countless complicated and subtle ways, but also she altered deeply in her attitude towards me. She refused, indeed, to be bland until the cause of her perturbation was removed.

How adorable she was in the seasons when she yearned

for love! Many female cats in this condition are over-
obtrusive, objectionably salacious. She became more affectionate, more gracious, and her tender little love-sighs
were very ingratiating. The first time she " called " for a
mate, a great tabby tom, the very fellow I have described
as an elevator-passenger, arrived from six flights below
and began to scratch on the outer door. What instinct is
this? How cats divine such a condition is more than I can
guess. Felines are not supposed to enjoy a highly developed
sense of smell and a calling female does not exude an
odour which is obvious to humans. Nor, in this particular
instance, so soft was her voice, could it be supposed that
she had been overheard. It has been stated by lepidopterists
that if a female butterfly of some rare species be exposed
in a cage in an open window, before many hours have
passed, males of this species will present themselves. At
this period another Persian cat resided in our apartment
house. On the unique occasion on which he secured his
liberty, like the tabby tom, he came directly to our door
and endeavoured to effect an entrance. Feathers, ensconced
behind the door, heard the scratching and challenged the
invaders, her manner completely altered. She growled.
She spit. The warmth of her nature had frozen. She was

chatte pour tout le monde, mais pour les chats tigresse!

Still she was a female and so manifestly destined for
motherhood. In a basket, following the fashion of the

aristocratic cat-world, in which the lady visits the gentleman, she was carried to a country-place on Long Island
where she was gently inserted into a cage already containing a eupeptic orange tabby sire who must have been
puzzled by her subsequent behaviour. She remained with
him for a week during which period she fought off his
attempted approaches with teeth and claws. Nevertheless,
when she returned home I hoped for progeny. When it
became evident that none might be expected, she was
sent back to her consort, again with no result.

In the middle of the hot summer of 1920, stupidly I
caused her to be sent back a third time. Yet I know very
well a cat will never do anything she does not wish to
do. She is quite willing to die to preserve her independence
of thought and action. Perhaps, in previous incarnations,
Feathers had done all the mating she considered necessary.
Perhaps she held a racial memory of the dreadful misalliances, the social errors, the sexual loosenesses, of her
mother and grandmothers. At any rate, on this third visit,
although exposed to the company of every male in the
cattery, for it was possible, we thought, that her refusal
had been dictated by her aversion for some particular cat,
she continued to defend her chastity. Her period of calling
passed and the lady in charge of the males asked me to
come out. Feathers was imprisoned in a cage near a
ferocious smoke who usually automatically dominated any
cat to whom he was introduced. He was twice as large

as Feathers. As I entered the room she was crouching on a shelf, but she rose, arched her back, waved her tail, and purred a greeting. She was begging me to take her away, but I did not understand. She was very thin: the most nervous cat I have ever known, she had not been eating well in this new environment. The smoke ventured a step towards her. With a well-aimed blow at his head, she contrived to throw him off his balance and the shelf. Like a villain in a melodrama foiled in his peccancy, he cringed on the floor. Still I did not understand.

The woman, who seemed to feel that her breeder's honour was at stake, begged me — in complete good faith, I am sure — to leave Feathers with her for another two weeks. If she remains with the cats until she calls again, she will perhaps learn to know them, was her specious argument. Unfortunately, I heeded it and bade farewell to Feathers. Did she plead with me with her eyes as I went away or, in recalling the scene later, did I imagine this? Rather, probably, she sank into a hopeless lassitude, hopeless of making any impression on my stupidity, hopeless of making me understand her at the crucial moment. Probably she turned her head away and resigned herself to her fate, dedicating herself to death.

The weather was cruelly warm, not hot and dry, but unbearably humid. Showers were frequent and one night, during a terrific thunderstorm, I lay awake, thinking how terrified Feathers must be. The end came a few days later, on a Sunday morning. In response to a telephone call I hurried to her, a long tedious journey of an hour. When I arrived, she was lying on her side, panting in the last breaths she was to take. A film was forming over her eyes.

III

For two years, save for those brief visits to Long Island, I had never been separated from Feathers. She had sat with me at breakfast and while I was writing. Her fine, intelligent eyes, her repose, her graceful beauty, her silence, and her mystery had become a part of my life, a part that I found I could do very ill without, a part that no other creature has supplied.

More, she represented a period, a period of two years, and it became increasingly difficult to recall any episode of these years divorced from her personality. It is seemingly simple, such a companionship, depending on scarcely more than mere propinquity, a few actions, a touch of the cold, moist nose, a soft paw against the cheek, a greeting at the door, a few moments of romping, a warm soft ball of fur curled on the knee, or a long stare. It is thus that the sympathy between men and animals expresses itself, but interwoven, and collectively, these details evoke an emotion which it is very difficult even for time to destroy.

July 22, 1921.

A NOTE ON BREAKFASTS

A NOTE ON BREAKFASTS

Breakfast is the most personal meal of the day. It requires, therefore, the most careful consideration. Luncheon, in the city at any rate, is a hasty, chatty meal, shared with intimates. At dinner it is possible that one may sit down with comparative strangers — comparative in the sense that you have been introduced to them in the drawing-room only a moment before — provided the cocktails have been sufficiently powerful. Assuredly, overlooking the idiosyncrasies of personal taste, it is a matter of indifference what one eats at these later repasts. At breakfast, on the contrary, the nature of food and of companions is of paramount importance.

Everything depends, of course, on the habitual mood of your awakening. There are those who bound out of bed whistling, or singing lustily, the latest popular tune. This sort of person demands a cold shower and indulges in chamber-athletics. To him, a heavy breakfast with several courses will not seem abhorrent. To him, who imbibes cheer and health and life from the morning air, it will not be unpleasing to share the table with friends or relatives. This fellow is an excellent choice for a week-end house-party, provided it is convenient to offer him a room and bath to himself.

SACRED AND PROFANE MEMORIES

The individual who awakes with a bad taste in his mouth and no conversation is indubitably more prevalent. He turns over several times and rearranges the sheets and pillows before he is able to invoke even enough energy to press a button on his bed-table. When his coffee is brought to him on a tray he regards it languidly. The first sip, he endures; the second is slightly more agreeable; in time, he drains the cup and pours out another. At the end of half-an-hour, he feels sufficiently human to read his morning mail or to scan the headlines of his newspaper.

Between these two extreme types there lie, naturally, many variations. For myself, I may confess that I never take cold baths and I never sing. It is equally true that I never sing before dinner. Nevertheless, my breakfast manners are by no means steadfast. I have discovered them to be prescribed by environment.

In my home in the Middle West it was the unhappy custom to serve breakfast for all the members of the family, fully dressed, at seven-thirty. I conformed to this custom, although not without hearty protest, until, at the age of nineteen, I went away to college. To approach the table at that hour properly clad, for dressing-gowns were forbidden, demanded rising a full thirty minutes earlier. In a futile attempt to bring about this desirable end, my mother used to call me when she herself arose. This warning was usually unavailing. I found myself able to reply to the call in my sleep and then to doze more deeply again, with the result that frequently the family were half through their rations before I made an appearance in the dining-room. To miss the whole of this meal was not a simple feat, as the summons was repeated at intervals and breakfast at our house continued for nearly an hour. First, there was fruit, preserved or fresh, then a breakfast food, usually oatmeal, for this was before the day when it became fashionable to christen cereal foods after Pullman cars, then the principal course, sausage, or bacon and eggs, or fried steak, together with potatoes, often boiled and smothered in cream. An extraordinary collection of pots appeared on the table in front of my mother: a pot of coffee, a pot of tea, and a pot of postum, to satisfy the diversity in taste for beverages on the part of the several members of my family. Until I was fifteen I added to the confusion by drinking hot milk. After, or during the meat course, pancakes, buckwheat, corn, or wheat, were served, although occasionally popovers, or Sally Lunns, or doughnuts were substituted for these. Such were the breakfasts I was brought up on and which I have never eaten since, save when I have revisited my birthplace.

On my first morning at the University of Chicago I lonelily awoke to realize the fact that I must forage for my breakfast, as no meals were served in the hall where I slept. After dressing, therefore, I emerged to walk several blocks before I discovered an eating-house. Precisely the foods I was accustomed to at home were on the bill of fare, but the prices alarmed me. How could I afford to pay thirty-five cents for bacon and eggs and then lay out an additional twenty cents for pancakes? My modest allowance did not seem to warrant such extravagance. I compromised on rolls, two fried eggs, and coffee. A few days later, after I had accumulated an acquaintance or two, I learned that it was the thing to sit on a stool in a snug little cabin near the athletic field and crack jokes with the untidy old woman who prepared the rude fare. It was here that I first consumed sinkers and, curiously enough, from that moment on, I never again suffered from the indigestion which had caused me so much pain in my extreme youth. Thereafter, my college breakfasts varied. On bright, spring mornings it was pleasant to sit before a table in the pavilion in Jackson Park. Later, in my fraternity house we demanded what we wanted when we wanted it from Desdemona Sublett, who sold bricks for the projected new African M. E. Church for four or five years.

I began my newspaper days with an early shift. Working on an afternoon paper, I was obliged to report at four in the morning to clip the rival papers and arrange the strings of stories in a convenient manner to meet the eye of the city editor, who arrived at seven. To prepare myself for this task, at three-forty-five I hied myself to one of the few restaurants in the loop open so early. There each morning I munched two large pieces of apple pie and drank a great cup of worse coffee than any I have ever sampled before or since. I could, I believe, eat anything in those days, and often did.

Three years later, at the age of twenty-six, I was discharged from the Chicago American for "lowering the tone of the Hearst newspapers" — I am quoting from the managing editor's note to me. Feeling certain that I had accomplished all that was possible in the West, I took a train for New York where, almost immediately, I found employment on the Times. Here, I was not obliged to report for duty until eleven. For the first time in my life, therefore, I enjoyed the luxury of lying in bed in the morning. During my second year in New York I moved into the Maison Favre on Seventh Avenue, where Madame Favre, often in a dressing-sacque, presided in the evening over a good, old-fashioned table d'hôte. Bottles of wine, furnished free with the dinner — and the dinner in those days cost seventy-five cents — stood on the tables and the conversation was coevally referred to as bohemian. The phrase went that you could cut the smoke with a knife. It was also considered clever to remark from time to time, So this is Paris! Occasionally Lotta Faust, the famous half-back of her time, or some minor opera singer from the Metropolitan, enlivened the evening for me merely by her presence. Well, at the Maison Favre — which deserves a whole story to itself; some day I may take the trouble to write it down — as I have said, I lay in bed until late in the morning, when good old Annie, incongruously Irish, at a certain set hour brought up my breakfast, consisting invariably of shirred eggs, chocolate, and croissants. She rapped gently before she deposited the tray on the floor outside my door. If I did not heed the tap immediately, ten to one Madame's little black-and-tan, Fifi, ate the breakfast and another had to be provided for me.

Petit déjeuner at the Maison Favre served to prepare me for Paris where it is the excellent tradition to sip chocolate or coffee and crunch croissants in bed, but, inexplicably, when I went to London, I began, quite avidly, to enjoy English breakfasts. In the public dining-room of my hotel I ate kippers or bloaters and followed them up with a healthy helping of meat and eggs, accompanied by orange marmalade, a conserve I cannot even look at anywhere else. This benign adaptability is a quality I still possess. Invariably, in London, I wake up in the morning with a good appetite. In a Munich pension, discovering the coffee and chocolate to be indifferent and the beer heavenly, it occurred to me to sample Münchener as a breakfast beverage, and thereafter I followed this system with regularity. I did not, reflection informs me, invent this plan. Some years earlier, in Chicago, I had been assigned in my capacity as reporter to meet Sarah Bernhardt at the railway station. The actress, fresh — or weary — from a South American tour, had disembarked in New York and caught a train leaving directly for the West, where she proposed to open one of her farewell American tours. If memory serves, she undertook five more. I still recall the crowd in the station, the diva's exit from her private car, all velvets and furs and carnations. Leaning on the arm of one of her comrades, she bestowed on the bystanders her alarming smile with the gums exposed, at the same time seductive and repulsive, and then tottered up the platform to clasp the hand of the engineer who had driven her safely to her destination, all this to the accompaniment of innumerable flashlight explosions. Then, entering a vehicle, Madame was borne to the Auditorium, a hotel erected in the purest Style Benjamin Harrison, where I, together with a half-dozen other newspaper men, rejoined her. How do you like America? What is your favourite city in the United States? All the usual questions were asked and answered in the usual way. Now, her manager entered, breathless. The theatre, at which she was announced to appear in a different play each night, and for two matinees, was sold out for the week. Would Madame consent to play matinees on the five remaining afternoons? . . . But yes, was her reply. You know my terms, so much a performance — in advance. , . . Splendid! cried the impresario. We shall endeavour to make it easy for Madame. What would Madame wish to play? Some lighter piece, perhaps, on these extra days? . . . Sarah, the divine, shrugged her shoulders. Don't annoy me with business details, she urged. You know I have a repertory of fifty dramas. Announce anything you like and let me know in time to get my dresses to the theatre. . . . During this conversation and the ensuing interviews with the journalists, Madame consumed her breakfast: two poached eggs, a porterhouse steak, fried potatoes, and *two bottles of Budweiser*.

I have a vague memory of having sampled Edam cheese at eight A.M. in Amsterdam some fifteen years ago, but continental breakfasts in later years have left a more enduring and a more æsthetic impression. It is pleasant to recall the breakfasts at the Villa Allegra outside of Florence, where I rose at my desire and strolled out into the garden to gaze over the balustrade towards the lovely hills, given form and colour by the gnarled olive-trees with their sage-green foliage, and the funereal, heaven-pointing cypresses — I am reminded, with some amusement, of the fact recorded by Bernard Shaw that a scene-painter for Augustin Daly painted these trees a lettuce-green for a production of The Two Gentlemen of Verona. I listened to the bells tolling softly from the invisible campanili in the city below. In the garden itself, where daphnes and oleanders and gardenias blossomed, a white peacock strutted and a monkey screamed. Presently, my morning revery was interrupted by the appearance of Vittorio, obsequious and sardonic, bearing a tray and demanding where I would have it placed. Quite alone, I sat on a marble bench to enjoy my drip coffee, honey, and rolls in this curious confusion of nature and artifice, so like a stage-setting for an Oscar Wilde comedy. In English and American country-houses I have since frequently experienced a similar decorative solitude. I recall too an amusing episode in the garden of an inn on the mountain above Heidelberg where I was forced to compete with a swarm of bees for my food and, finally vanquished, ran laughing down the mountainside.

Perhaps the most titillating breakfasts of all are those of which one partakes before going to bed, the early dawn breakfasts at Pré Catalan in the Bois of Paris where it formerly was the fashion — and possibly still is: I have not been there at the proper hour for many years — to actually milk the cow to the astonishment of the intoxicated customers, or the breakfasts one eats at some hole in the wall off the Place Pigalle where sleepy women of the streets share snacks with their souteneurs before officially retiring. In New York, in the days before the war, unless one modestly repaired to Childs' for butter-cakes, Jack's was the rendez-vous for all the delightful people who like to stay up all night. Jack's did as flourishing a business at six in the morning as any other successful restaurant does at seven-thirty in the evening. Here newspaper men and actresses gobbled platters of scrambled eggs and tomatoes, garnished with Irish bacon, and washed down with good beer or Scotch highballs — unless they had acquired a taste for Bushnell's Irish whisky, which has an aroma like that of apple-blossoms. The stragglers from smart East Side parties also wandered in and, as people who stay up all night form a kind of club, and as no one who eats breakfast before he goes to bed objects to sharing it, there was a good deal of visiting from table to table. It was here that Vernon Castle, then engaged in "feeding" Lew Fields in The Girl Behind the Counter at the old Herald Square Theatre, executed amusing slight-of-hand tricks with table-knives. It was here that Monsieur de Max, remembering, perhaps, the tribulations of Œdipus Rex, glowered saturninely from a corner table. It was here that Frank O'Malley, who had recently created that masterpiece of journalistic spoofing, The Good Ship Wobble, in the Sun, was an inevitable figure. One night a soldier from one of the armouries rode his bewildered stallion into the rooms. One night Donald Evans, requisitioning a bowl of fresh blood, employed it to indite a sonnet on the table-cloth. Donald invariably breakfasted on six raw eggs and six cups of black coffee, as strong as he could get it made, which reminds me that Edgar Saltus has described another poet who breakfasted on foie gras and curaçao. Jack himself, grey-haired and grey-moustached, always immaculate in his evening clothes, a scarlet carnation in his button-hole, wandered about like the host of a yachting party, while the Irish waiters exchanged questionable pleasantries with the customers or occasionally formed a flying-wedge to bounce an obstreperous guest. Jack's only recently closed its doors for ever, but long ago prohibition and the passage of time had changed the character of the

A NOTE ON BREAKFASTS

place, although many of the identical waiters remained to the end to remind us that some things in life are stable. They became sadder eyed and less spry of limb, however, and it was a melancholy experience to observe their faces brighten whenever chance brought an old habitué back to his table.

May 26, 1925.

NOTES FOR AN AUTOBIOGRAPHY

NOTES FOR AN AUTOBIOGRAPHY

I cannot remember the time when I was not trying to write, often with no reasonable amount of skill. I think it would be true to state that I always wanted to write — although I also cherished other ambitions; at one period I craved a career as a concert pianist; at another, as a jockey — but I do not think at first it occurred to me that I wanted to write a book.

At the University of Chicago I contributed some really vile sketches to the Weekly and during the same period wrote a rather better letter or two for the Pulse, the monthly organ of the Cedar Rapids (Iowa) High School. Also at the University I specialized in English with Robert Morss Lovett, the best teacher I ever had and still my friend, William Vaughn Moody, and Robert Herrick. Herrick, I believe, was the first novelist I ever met and a hero to me for many years on this account.

My themes were pretty dreadful — I have retained some of them, probably the best: so I am not criticizing from memory — but my energy in creating them was enormous, and once or twice I almost hit on something in the way of an idea. My modest design was to prepare myself for a career on a newspaper. On leaving college, with a boost from

Sam Paquin, a fraternity brother, I easily satisfied this intention, joining the forces of Hearst's Chicago American. As the staff of this paper at this epoch included such brilliant reporters as Hugh Fullerton, Charles Finnegan, and Charlie Fitzmorris, the Chicago boy who beat Nelly Bly's record in a race around the world, and who afterwards became Chicago's Chief of Police, naturally I was offered but scant opportunity to write. I was sent out to gather information regarding "stories" which I telephoned in and the accounts that appeared in the paper were the work of these "rewrite" men. I was also deputed to fetch photographs of persons in the news and was so successful at this humble occupation that I was kept at it interminably, and only actually broke away from it, and the kindly tyranny of Moses Koenigsberg, the city editor, when I left for New York in 1906.

My first home in New York was a large room at 39 West Thirty-ninth Street where Sinclair Lewis occupied an adjoining chamber, but I cannot describe him as the second novelist I met because at that time he was yet to publish his first book. From the Chicago American I went to the New York Times, but previously I had sold a paper on Richard Strauss's Salome, produced during that season at the Metropolitan Opera House, to the Broadway Magazine. It appeared in the January 1907 number of that periodical. Theodore Dreiser was the editor who ordered and accepted this paper. He was, I fancy, the second novelist I encountered. I saw him frequently at this period — six years after the publication of Sister Carrie — and we discussed the possibility of my writing further articles. One about Columbia University was ordered, I believe, and perhaps written, but certainly not published. On the staff of the magazine was a picturesque young man called Harris Merton Lyon, the De Maupassant, Jr., of Dreiser's Twelve Men. Shortly after I sold my paper on Salome to Dreiser, I was engaged as assistant to Mr. Richard Aldrich on the music department of the New York Times. By this time I was thoroughly convinced that I wanted to be a music critic and write for the magazines. It was not long before I had satisfied both these ambitions. I also served for nearly a year as Paris correspondent of the New York Times. It had not yet occurred to me that I would write a book.

In September 1913, I joined the New York Press as dramatic critic. In June 1914, Mr. Frank Munsey, the eccentric owner of this newspaper, decided to dispense with my services. A few months later he decided to dispense with the paper itself. After a trip abroad and a short experience as the editor of a dying magazine of parts which published articles about Gertrude Stein and early poems by Wallace Stevens, I recalled a remark made to me by Mr. George Moore, the third novelist I met. I had originally encountered Mr. Moore at Jacques Blanche's in Paris and he had talked so well and I had remembered so much of what he said that afterwards I had recorded the conversation.

When, later, I had shown him this paper, he had demanded of me: Why don't you make this the nucleus for a book of essays? . . . Now, in the spring of 1915, with no occupation, I began to consider Mr. Moore's casual suggestion, also bearing in mind the sapient advice of Jack Reed, who had read a good many of my articles: Why don't you try to write the way you talk?

It happened, however, that aside from my paper on Mr. Moore — which, by the way, has not appeared in a book to this day — I believed my best writing dealt with music. It was therefore seven musical articles that I chose to work over to form the contents of my first book, Music After the Great War. One of these, Massenet and Women, had been printed in the New Music Review as early as February 1913. After the book was typed, it seemed reasonable to me that a music publisher would be the most appropriate person with whom to entrust the manuscript. I had often encountered Mr. Rudolph Schirmer at the Opera House and so it was quite naturally to him that I handed my typewritten pages. He received them without cordiality, but, on the advice of his reader, the manuscript was immediately accepted and published the same year: 1915. Among others Mr. H. L. Mencken thought well of Music After the Great War and said so at some length in the Smart Set.

If my first book was born without difficulty, my second book was rejected, and, as a matter of fact, it has never been published to this day.[1] It is the only book I have ever written which has not been accepted for immediate publication. Its title was Pastiches et Pistaches, a title I afterwards employed to head a series of random notes written for the Reviewer. Among the thirteen publishers who rejected it was Alfred A. Knopf. Unlike the others, however, Mr. Knopf was curious enough to read my first book and interested enough in that to invite me to come to see him. At that time, he occupied a single room, with a cubby-hole for a boy, in an office building on West Forty-second Street. He resembled a Persian prince and certainly behaved like one. His suggestion was that as I knew a good deal about music and seemed to be able to write about it, for the moment I should stick to that general subject. The result of this encouraging conversation was the planning and execution of Music and Bad Manners, issued in 1916 by Mr. Knopf, who has been my publisher ever since.

In the winter of 1920 I conceived the idea which led to the composition of Peter Whiffle. When it was completed I took the manuscript to Mr. Knopf. I had not told him that I was writing a novel. As a matter of fact I do not believe I knew that I was writing a novel. However, after

[1] The separate papers in this collection have, of course, for the most part been published. Some of them are included in this volume.

it appeared, the reviewers began to declare that it was a novel and so, to my astonishment, I found myself a novelist and sat down to write, with the greatest ease, The Blind Bow-Boy.

In this brief account of my early adventures in the art of writing, I have not referred to my first appearance as a player of chamber-music (witnesses still live who have heard me perform the piano parts in violin and piano sonatas by Richard Strauss, César Franck, and Edvard Grieg) nor have I dwelt on my respective débuts as actor and composer, careers which I was not encouraged to follow.

June 4, 1930.

BIBLIOGRAPHY

BIBLIOGRAPHY

Carl
Van Vechten

BOOKS

MUSIC AFTER THE GREAT WAR (1915)
MUSIC AND BAD MANNERS (1916) *Out of print*
INTERPRETERS AND INTERPRETATIONS (1917) *Out
  of print*
THE MERRY-GO-ROUND (1918) *Out of print*
THE MUSIC OF SPAIN (1918) [1] *Out of print*
IN THE GARRET (1920) *Out of Print*
INTERPRETERS (1920) *Out of print*
THE TIGER IN THE HOUSE (1920) [1]
PETER WHIFFLE: His Life and Works (1922) [1]
THE BLIND BOW-BOY (1923) [1]
THE TATTOOED COUNTESS (1924) [1]
RED (1925)
FIRECRACKERS (1925) [1]
EXCAVATIONS (1926)

[1] Published in England.

BIBLIOGRAPHY

NIGGER HEAVEN (1926) [1 2 3 4 5 7 8 9 10]
SPIDER BOY (1928) [1 2 4 5 6]
FEATHERS (1930)
PARTIES (1930) [1]
SACRED AND PROFANE MEMORIES (1932)

PAMPHLETS AND BROADSHEETS

SYMPHONY SOCIETY BULLETIN; Volume IV; Nos. I–VIII (1910–11)

WHY AND WHAT (an advertising pamphlet, signed Atlas, 1914)

MARGUERITE D'ALVAREZ (a broadsheet, 1920)

PAUL ROBESON (a program note, 1925)

TAYLOR GORDON AND J. ROSAMOND JOHNSON (a program note, 1925)

ELLEN GLASGOW (1927)

Preface to the catalogue of an exhibition by Robert W. Chanler at the Valentine Gallery (February 1929)

KEEP A-INCHIN' ALONG, in the program of the N. A. A. C. P. benefit at the Forrest Theatre, New York (December 8, 1929)

[1] Published in England.
[2] In French.
[3] In German.
[4] In Swedish.
[5] In the Tauchnitz edition.
[6] In Danish.
[7] In Italian.
[8] In Czechoslovakian.
[9] In Polish.
[10] In Esthonian.

BIBLIOGRAPHY

A broadsheet announcing THE NEGRO MOTHER, by
Langston Hughes (September 1931)

MR. VAN VECHTEN HAS WRITTEN PREFACES FOR
THE FOLLOWING BOOKS:

SOPHIE, by Philip Moeller (1919)
A LETTER WRITTEN IN 1837 BY MORGAN LEWIS
FITCH (privately printed, 1919)
LORDS OF THE HOUSETOPS (1921)
KITTENS, by Svend Fleuron (1922)
IN A WINTER CITY, by Ouida (The Modern Library,
1923)
MY MUSICAL LIFE, by N. A. Rimsky-Korsakoff
(1923) [1]
PRANCING NIGGER, by Ronald Firbank (1924)
THE LORD OF THE SEA, by M. P. Shiel (1924)
A BIBLIOGRAPHY OF CARL VAN VECHTEN, by Scott
Cunningham (1924)
THE PRINCE OF WALES AND OTHER FAMOUS AMERI-
CANS, by Miguel Covarrubias (1925)
FIFTY DRAWINGS BY ALASTAIR (1925)
THE WEARY BLUES, by Langston Hughes (1926)
THE AUTOBIOGRAPHY OF AN EX-COLORED MAN, by
James Weldon Johnson (1927)
BORN TO BE, by Taylor Gordon (1929)

[1] Published in England.

BIBLIOGRAPHY

THE FOLLOWING BOOKS CONTAIN PAPERS BY MR. VAN VECHTEN:

THE BORZOI: 1920

WHEN WINTER COMES TO MAIN STREET, by Grant Overton (1922)

ET CETERA (1924)

THE BORZOI: 1925

ONCE AND FOR ALL (1929)

HENRY B. FULLER, compiled and edited by Anna Morgan (1929)

THE COLOPHON, Part III (October 1930)

MR. VAN VECHTEN IS THE COMPOSER OF:

FIVE OLD ENGLISH DITTIES (1904)